A.

Bl

FIVE SHORT PLAYS

BY TENNESSEE WILLIAMS

ACTING EDITION

★

★

DRAMATISTS
PLAY SERVICE
INC.

PUBLISHER'S NOTE

American Blues brings together five examples of the work of the man who has given our theatre *The Glass Menagerie* and *A Streetcar Named Desire*. Of these, two have already been published in collections, but three are here printed for the first time, *Ten Blocks on the Camino Real*, *The Case of the Crushed Petunias* and *The Dark Room*. Each of these pieces, in its own fashion, not only throws light on the work of one of the most original dramatic writers of our day, but offers a challenge to reader and director alike, and a chance to share a part of the author's vision of life.

In justice to Mr. Williams, we must point out that the inclusion of *The Case of the Crushed Petunias* in this little book is the result of a concession on his part. We have always liked this charming little fantasy, but Mr. Williams, on re-reading it at first, asked us to leave it out on the grounds that it was an early and immature piece. So we argued the point with him: suppose it was written a decade ago, that it was immature, and possibly not a play in a blues mood? It lacks the moving compassionate drive of *The Glass Menagerie*, of course, but it has merits of its own, merits of another, and a lighter, kind. We do not believe in rummaging too thoroughly through the workshop of any artist, but *The Case of the Crushed Petunias* has, we believe, a right to publication, and that is why we thought it worth while to persuade its author to let us publish it. We feel confident that the public will agree with us.

MOONY'S KID DON'T CRY [1]

MOONY .... A Workingman

JANE .... His Wife

MOONY'S KID .... (Not a speaking part)

SCENE: *Kitchen of a cheap three-room flat in the industrial section of a large American city.*
Stove and sink are eloquent of slovenly housekeeping. A wash-line, stretched across one corner of the room, is hung with diapers and blue work-shirts. Above the stove is nailed a placard, KEEP SMILING. The kitchen table supports a small artificial Christmas tree.

By far the most striking and attractive article in the room is a brand-new hobby-horse that stands stage Center. There is something very gallant, almost exciting, about this new toy. It is chestnut brown, with a long flowing mane, fine golden nostrils and scarlet upcurled lips. It looks like the very spirit of unlimited freedom and fearless assault.

As the curtain opens, the stage is dark except for a faint bluish light through the window- and door-panes. Offstage in the next room are heard smothered groans and creaking bedsprings.

JANE. (*Off-stage.*) Quit that floppin' around. It keeps me awake.
MOONY. Think I'm gettin' any sleep, do you?!
(SOUND: *more rattling.*)
JANE. Quiet! You'll wake the kid up.
MOONY. The kid, the kid! What's more important, him sleeping or me? Who brings home the pay-check, me or the kid? (*Pause.*)
JANE. I'll get up an' fix you a cup of hot milk. That'll quiet you down maybe. (MOONY *grumbles incoherently.* JANE *pads softly on-*

[1] Copyright, 1940, by Tennessee Williams.

stage, into the kitchen. She is amazingly slight, like a tiny mandarin, enveloped in the ruins of a once gorgeously-flowered Japanese silk kimono. As she prepares the hot milk for MOONY, *she pads about the kitchen in a pair of men's felt bedroom slippers which she has a hard time keeping on her small feet. She squeezes the kimono tight about her chest, and shivers. Coughs once or twice. Glances irritably at the alarm-clock on window-sill, which says nearly four o'clock in the morning.* JANE *is still young, but her pretty, small-featured face has a yellowish, unhealthy look. Her temples and nostrils are greased with Vick's Vap-o-Rub and her dark hair is tousled.)*

JANE. *(Strident whisper.)* What for? I'll bring yer milk in. (SOUND: *scraping of furniture and heavy footsteps.)* That's it, be sure you wake the kid up—clumsy ox! (MOONY *appears in the doorway, a strongly-built young workingman about twenty-five years old. He blinks his eyes and scowls irritably as he draws on his flannel shirt and stuffs it under the belt of his corduroy pants.)* It's that beer-drinkin'. Makes gas on yer stomach an' keeps yuh from sleepin'.

MOONY. Aw, I had two glasses right after dinner.

JANE. Two a them twenty-six ounces!—Quit that trampin' around, for Christ's sake! Can't you set still a minute?

MOONY. Naw, I feel like I got to be moving.

JANE. Maybe you got high blood-pressure.

MOONY. Naw, I got a wild hair. This place's give me the jitters. You know it's too damn close in here. Can't take more'n six steps in any direction without coming smack up against another wall. *(Half grinning.)* I'd like to pick up my axe and swing into this wall —— Bet I could smash clean through it in a couple of licks!

JANE. Moony! Why didn't I marry an ape an' go live in the zoo?

MOONY. I don't know. (JANE *pours the steaming milk into a blue cup.)*

JANE. Set down an' drink that. Know what time it is? Four o'clock in the morning!

MOONY. Four o'clock, huh? *(He continues to move restlessly about.)* Yeah. Soon ole fact'ry whistle be blowin'. Come on, you sonovaguns! Git to work!—Old Dutchman be standin' there with his hands on his little pot-belly, watchin' 'em punch in their cards. "Hi, dere, Moony," he says. "Late agin, huh? Vot you tink dis iss maybe, an afdernoon tea?" That's his joke. You know a Dutchman always has one joke that he keeps pluggin' at. An' that's his. Ev'ry morning the same damn thing ——

JANE. Yeah? Well ——

MOONY. "Ha, ha, Moony," he says, "you been out star-gazin' las' night! How many vas dere, Moony? How man stars vas dere out las' night? Ha, ha, *ha!*" —— (*Strides over to the window—flings it up.*)

JANE. Put that back down! I ain't got a stitch a clothes on under this.

MOONY. I'll say to him, "Sure, I seen 'em las' night. But not like they was in Ontario, not by a long shot, Mister." Grease-bubbles! That's what they look most like from here. Why, up in the North Woods at night ——

JANE. (*Impatiently.*) The North Woods! Put that thing down!

MOONY. Okay. (*Obeys.*)

JANE. Here. Drink yer milk. You act like a crazy man, honest to Jesus you do!

MOONY. Okay. Would that give the Dutchman a laugh!

JANE. What would? You better be careful.

MOONY. He'll go all over the plant—tell the boys what Moony said this morning—said he'd seen the stars las' night but not like they was in Ontario when he was choppin' down the big timber.

JANE. Yes, you'll give him a swell impression with talk of that kind. I'm dog-tired. (*Pours herself some of the steaming milk.*)

MOONY. Ever seen the St. Lawrence river?

JANE. Naw, I've seen wet diapers, that's all, for so long that ——!

MOONY. That's what I'll ask the Dutchman. I'll ask him if he's ever seen the St. Lawrence river.

JANE. (*Glancing at him suspiciously.*) What would you ask him that for?

MOONY. She's big. See? She's nearly as big and blue as the sky is, an' the way she flows is straight north. You ever heard of that, Jane? A river that flowed straight north?

JANE. (*Indifferently, as she sips her hot milk.*) No.

MOONY. Only river I ever known of that flowed north!

JANE. Emma says a drop of paregoric would keep his bowels from runnin' off like that. I think I'll try it next time.

MOONY. We was talkin' about it one day an' Spook says it's because the earth is curved down that way toward the Arctic Circle! (*Grins.*)

JANE. What?

MOONY. He said that's why she flows north ——

JANE. Who cares?

MOONY. Naw, the Dutchman don't, neither. That's why I tell him. Makes it funny, see? I'll tell him she's big, damn big, an' they call her the Lake of a Thousand Islands!

JANE. He'll say you're crazy. He'll tell you to go an' jump in it!

MOONY. Sure he will. That's what makes it funny. I'll tell him she's big an' blue as the sky is, with firs an' pines an' tamaracks on both sides of her fillin' the whole God-beautiful air with—the smell of— Hot milk, huh? Wouldn't that give the Dutchman a laugh!— Hot milk at four o'clock in the morning!—He'd go all over the plant an' tell the boys that Moony must have his liddle hot milk at night when he goes bye-bye with the Sandman.

JANE. Louise Krause's husband commenced sayin' such things an' they called out the ambulance squad. Right now he's in a strait-jacket in the psychopathic ward an' when Louise went up to see him he didn't remember who she was even! Demen-shuh *pre-cox* they called it! (MOONY *seizes cup and dashes milk to floor.*) Moony!—What d'yuh think yuh're doin', yuh big lug? Sloppin' good milk on the floor!

MOONY. Hot milk, huh?

JANE. Oh, dear Christ! You an' your kid, what a mess you both are! No wonder they all make fun of you down at the plant. The way that you act there's only one word for it—crazy! (MOONY *snorts indignantly.*) Yes, crazy! Crazy is the only word for your actions!

MOONY. Crazy, huh? Sure them apes think I'm nuts. I'll tell you why; it's because I got some original ideas about some things.

JANE. Original, yeah, you're so stinkin' original it ain't even funny! Believe me if I'd a-known ——

MOONY. I look at things diff'runt—(*Struggling for self-justifica-tion.*)—that's all. Other guys—you know how it is—they don't care. They eat, they drink, they sleep with their women. What the hell do they care? The sun keeps rising and Saturday night they get paid!—Okay, okay, okay! Some day they kick off. What of it? They got kids to grow up an' take their places. Work in the plant. Eat, drink, sleep with their women—an' get paid Saturday night!—But me —— (*He laughs bitterly.*) My God, Jane, I want something more than just that!

8

JANE. What more do you want, you poor fool? There *ain't* nothing more than just that —— Of course if you was rich and could afford a big house and a couple of limoozines ——

MOONY. (*Disgustedly.*) Aw, you—you don't even get what I'm aimin' at, Jane! (*He sinks wearily down on checkered linoleum and winds arms about his knees.*) You never could get it. It's something that ain't contagious.

JANE. Well, I'm glad for that. I'd rather have small-pox.

MOONY. I found a guy once that did. An old duck up on the river. He got his back hurt, couldn't work, was waiting to be shipped home —— We got drunk one night an' I spilled how I felt about things. He said, "Sure. You ain't satisfied. Me neither. We want something more than what life ever gives to us, kid."

JANE. It gives you what you can get.

MOONY. Oh, I dunno. I look at my hands sometimes, I look an' I look at 'em. God, but they look so damn funny!

JANE. You look at your hands! Such crap!

MOONY. They're so kind of empty an' useless! You get what I mean? I feel like I oughta be doin' something with these two han's of mine besides what I'm doin' now—runnin' bolts through an everlastin' chain!

JANE. Here's something. (*Flings him a dish rag.*) Try holdin' this for a change in them wonderful hands —— Mop that milk up off the floor!

MOONY. (*Idly twisting the cloth.*) An' then sometimes I think it ain't my han's that're empty. It's something else inside me that is.

JANE. Yeh, it's probably yer brain. Will you get that milk swabbed up?

MOONY. It's already swabbed! (*Rises and stretches.*) Moony's a free agent. He don't give a damn what anyone thinks. Live an' die, says Moony, that's all there is to it! (*He tosses the wet rag back to the sink.*)

JANE. (*Straightening things in a lifeless, ineffectual way.*) Believe me, if I'd a-known you was gonna turn out this way, I'd a-kept my old job. I'd a-said to Mr. O'Connor, "Sure thing! Go ahead an' get me that chinchilla coat."

MOONY. Sure you would. I know it, sweetheart.

JANE. (*Beginning to sniffle.*) What's the good of a girl trying to keep herself straight? The way things turns out, a good proposition like Mr. O'Connor could offer would be the best thing. But no! I had such delusions about cha! You talked so swell! You made such a lovely impression that time we first met!

MOONY. Lots of water's run under the bridge since then.

JANE. Yeah.

MOONY. When was that, Jane? How long ago was it?

JANE. Ten months; an' it seems ten years!

MOONY. Ten months. And how old's the kid? One month? Exactly one month?

JANE. (*Furiously.*) You've got a nerve to say that! As if it was me that insisted, that couldn't wait even until we'd ——

MOONY. Naw, it wasn't your fault. It was nature got hold of us both that night, Jane. Yuh remember? The Paradise dance-hall down on the water-front, huh? My first night in town after six months up in the woods. You had on a red silk dress. Yuh remember? Cut down sorta low in front. Hah, you was real pretty then—your hair frizzed up in the back in a thousan' or so little curls that I could just barely poke my littlest finger through!

JANE. (*Falling under a nostalgic spell.*) Yeah. (*Her face softens.*) I useter have it done ev'ry Satiddy night. Mamie said she never seen hair that could take such a curl!

MOONY. (*With sly cruelty.*) Yeh, that's how it was—them curls— an' the red silk dress—it was nature got hold us both that night, huh, Jane?

JANE. (*Suspecting an innuendo.*) What d'yuh mean by that?

MOONY. The way you pressed up against me when we was dancing —that was nature, wasn't it, Jane? And when they played "Roses of Picardy" an' the lights was turned out—we was dancin' real slow—we was almost standin' still—your breath was so warm on my neck, so warm—you had on a kind of perfume ——

JANE. Perfume? Oh, yes. Narcissus perfume!—Mr. O'Connor give it to me for my birthday.

MOONY. Yeah, narcissus, that's it—narcissus! An' what was it, Jane, you whispered in my ear?

JANE. (*Indignantly.*) *Me* whispered? It was *you* that whispered, not *me!*

MOONY. Was it? Maybe it was. You didn't have to say nothin', the way you danced was enough!—Anyhow, I got hooked.

JANE. (*Furiously.*) Hooked! Hooked?! You dare to say such a thing?!

MOONY. Yes, I was hooked all right. Narcissus perfume, little curls, an' a low-cut dress. Makin' me think that holdin' you in my arms an' waltzin' aroun' a two-bit arch-acher was better'n holdin' an axe in my two han's up in the North woods an' choppin' down big trees!

JANE. (*Choking.*) You—you ——! (*Covers her face.*)

MOONY. (*A little less harshly.*) Aw, well, I don't mean that I'm—sorry about it—exactly . . .

JANE. (*Brokenly.*) How didja mean it, I'd liketa know then?

MOONY. (*Pacing about the kitchen.*) Oh, I dunno, I dunno! (*Suddenly stops and catches* JANE *in his arms.*) People say things, things happen! What does it mean? I dunno. Seems to me like a crazy man, deaf, dumb, and blind, could have put together a better kind of a world than this is! (*He kisses* JANE'S *bare shoulder where the kimono has slipped down a little.*) Let's get out of it, honey!

JANE. (*Sniffling.*) Out of it? What d'yuh mean?

MOONY. (*Violently.*) Chuck it all; the whole damn thing—that's what!

JANE. You mean —— (*She backs away from him, frightened.*) Kill ourselves?

MOONY. (*Laughing impatiently.*) Well, no—no! I don't wanta *die!* I wanta *live!*—What I mean is, get out of this place, this lousy town —— Smoke, whistles, plants, factories, buildings, buildings, buildings!—You get caught in 'em, you never can find your way out!—So break away quick while you can!—Get out where it's clean an' there's space to swing an axe in! An' some time to swing it! Oh, God, Jane, don't you see—see—*see?*

JANE. Yes. You mean hop a freight train! (*Laughs mockingly.*)

MOONY. Sure that's it if you want to! Tell the Dutchman good-bye—tell him to kiss my Aunt Fanny!

JANE. (*Hysterically.*) Me with the baby an' my infection of the breast—you with your axe! We'll spend Christmas in a box-car, won't we, Moony?

MOONY. You bet!—Me with my axe, we'll chop a way through this world!

JANE. (*Laughing.*) What a joke,—what a lovely *scream* that is!

MOONY. A joke, huh? Who said a joke?

JANE. Moony, Moony, my great big wonderful man! He'll cut a way—(*Chokes with laughter.*)—through this world!

MOONY. (*Getting sore.*) Make fun of me, huh?

11

JANE. Moony they call him! Down at the plant it's Moony this, Moony that! All of them making fun of my man, laughing at him right to his face, and he's so damn dumb he don't know it! They got your number, they have! The Dutchman's got your number. You're just a star-gazer! You oughta put up your tent an' tell fortunes! Oh, you damn fool! If it wasn't so funny I could cry, I could cry! You with your axe! We'll spend Christmas in a box-car! You'll chop a way through the world! Ha, ha! You with your axe? What a *scream!*—Couldn't even chop down a kid's Christmas tree—I hadda buy one at the dime store! And that horse —— (*She gets breathless and hoarse from laughter.*) That's the best one! Brings home a five-dollar hobby-horse when we ain't even got money enough to pay the hospital bill!

MOONY. I lied to you, Jane. I paid ten-fifty for that little horse.

JANE. (*Aghast.*) Ten-fifty? You—you —— No, it's not possible —even *you* couldn't ——

MOONY. It was worth more than that!

JANE. Worth more? More?! Worth ——! (*She is breathless.*)

MOONY. Sure it was!

JANE. Buys a ten-fifty hobby-horse for a month-old baby —— They lock people up for doing less than that!

MOONY. Aw, he'll grow up to it, Jane. (*He is a little abashed.*) I had one o' these things when I was a kid.

JANE. You musta got thrown off it an' landed on your head!

MOONY. Naw, Dad got drunk one Saturday night, an' bought me one at a junk-shop. Mother, she felt like you did, when he come home with it. But me, I was nuts about it. Him an' me, both, we got on the horse—him in back, me in front—an' sang "Ride a Cock-horse to Danbury Cross."

JANE. Oh, my God! Now I know where you got it. He was a lunatic, too!

MOONY. Naw, he was smart. He run out on us.

JANE. Run out on your mother, he did? Well, it's not surprising!

MOONY. I never heard of him since.

JANE. Well—he probably got what was coming to him.

MOONY. (*With quick rage.*) Better than what I got!

JANE. What you got?

MOONY. A skinny yellow cat—that's what I got!

JANE. (*Gasping.*) Oh ——! God oughta strike you down dead for saying a thing like that!

MOONY. Yeah? I say it again—a yellow cat,—a skinny yellow cat! (*JANE strikes him across face. MOONY becomes like a mad animal. Roars and lunges forward—clutches JANE by throat. They grapple fiercely for several moments. Then JANE collapses in his arms.*)

JANE. (*Weakly.*) Lemme go—please—for God's sake!

MOONY. (*Disgustedly.*) Ahhh—yer too soft! (*He flings her away from him. She falls against interior door, and hangs onto knob and edge of sink for support. MOONY hitches his belt undecidedly. He can't look at JANE's dazed face. He is ashamed, but still defiant.*) I'm leaving you now—get that? I'm checking out. You can tell the Dutchman to give you my pay—owes me three days —— Time an' a ha'f for Saturday —— (*Gives his belt final hitch, and moves over to peg where his lumberman's jacket is hanging. He gives JANE a swift furtive glance as he puts on the jacket, says: "H'mmm!" Stoops down to pick up his axe. Feels the blade with a gingerly pride. Takes awkward practice swing. Eyes glow triumphantly to life. He looks again at JANE like an escaped animal at a cage. She does not move. She stares at him with hurt animal eyes. MOONY spits on his fingers, runs them along the axe blade again. Hoarsely.*) Pretty sharp, still. Good ole axe—h'mmm! (*He starts toward the outer door.*) Maybe I'll—see you sometime—Jane. (*Fumbles with latch.*) So long. (*He jerks door open. Stands on threshold.*) H'mmm. Feel that wind. Good an' clear tonight. A touch a frost in the air. An' them stars. Millions of 'em, huh? Quantity production, everything on a big scale,—that's God! Millions of stars—millions of people. Only He knew what to do with the stars. Stuck 'em up there in the sky to look pretty. But people—down here in the mud. Ugh, too many of 'em, God! They must have run away with you, I guess. Crawling over each other, snatching and tearing, living an' dying till the earth's just a big soup of dead bodies!—How did that happen? Gosh, it's sure funny! —Oh, well, what's the use? A man's gotta live his own life. Cut his own ways through the woods somehow —— (*The cold air sweeping into the room brings JANE out of her stupefaction. She slides to the floor and crawls toward MOONY like a half-crushed animal.*)

JANE. Moony!—(*Hoarsely.*)—You wouldn't walk out on me, honey? Me with the baby and my infection of the breast, and no money or nothing? (*MOONY turns toward her a tortured face. Snatches at his pockets and flings a few coins on the floor.*)

13

MOONY. Four bits! Tobacco money! Now you got the whole works —so good-bye!

JANE. Wait! (*She clutches his arm and her fury makes her inescapable.*) There's something you got to take with you! Your property, Moony—you might as well take it along!

MOONY. I got all I want.

JANE. No, you ain't. There's something else that goes with you. You just wait here for a second, I'll wrap it up for you —— (*Crosses quickly to door upstage.*)

MOONY. What the hell are you ——! (*He hesitates at the door. JANE quickly reappears with the baby in her arms.*)

JANE. Here! Here's your kid, Moony! Take him with you. Sure.— Go along, now, the *two* of you! (*Shoves baby into MOONY's unwilling arms.*) Me, I can't be bothered with no brats. I got to go back to work. O'Connor will give me my old job back. Sure he will. You two can go an' hop a freight an' spend Christmas in a box-car. Maybe you'll find your old man —— You'll have a swell time singing "Ride a Cock-horse" together! (*She laughs wildly and runs out of the room. MOONY gingerly holds the baby. Looks helplessly down at its face. Frowns. Swears under his breath. Finally slams the door shut.*)

MOONY. Another one of her lousy tricks! (*Baby starts crying.*) SHUT UP! (*Then more softly.*) Moony's kid don't cry! (*He smiles slightly and rocks the baby in his arms.*) Naw, Moony's kid don't cry. Grows up an' swings a big axe like his Daddy. Cuts his own way through the woods. (*He walks away from the door, completely absorbed now in the baby, and apparently forgetting that he ever had any intention of going away.*) Lookit the hobby-horse! (*Stands above the new toy.*) Santie Claus bought it for Moony's Kid. Ten-fifty it cost! See? How shiny it is! Nice, huh? Nice! What are you crying for? Daddy ain't going nowhere. Naw! —Daddy was only—fooling. . . .

SLOW CURTAIN

14

THE DARK ROOM [1]

CHARACTERS

MISS MORGAN

MRS. POCCIOTTI

LUCIO

SCENE: *For expediency the same set as in "Moony's Kid Don't Cry" may be used, with a few prop changes and general rearrangement to heighten effect of poverty.*
MISS MORGAN is pretty much a stock character: the neat, fussy spinster engaged in social service. She may be interpreted more or less sympathetically, as the producer desires.

MRS. POCCIOTTI is an avalanche of female flesh, swarthy Italian, her bulk emphasized by a ridiculously skimpy gray knit sweater, whose sleeves extend half-way down her forearms. Everything about her is heavy and deliberate except her eyes, which smolder and dart suspiciously.

MISS MORGAN. (*Seated at table with pencil and pad.*) Now your husband, Mrs. Pocciotti, just how long has he been unemployed?
MRS. POCCIOTTI. God knows how long.
MISS MORGAN. I'm afraid I'll have to have a more definite answer.
MRS. POCCIOTTI. (*Poking her broom under the stove.*) Musta been —1930 he got laid off.
MISS MORGAN. He has been unemployed ever since? For eight or nine years?
MRS. POCCIOTTI. For eight or nine years. No jobs.
MISS MORGAN. Was he—incapacitated—I mean—was anything *wrong* with your husband?

MRS. POCCIOTTI. His head was no good. He couldn't remember no more.

MISS MORGAN. I see. His mind was affected. Now has he received hospital or institutional treatment of any kind during this period, Mrs. Pocciotti?

MRS. POCCIOTTI. He comes home, he goes back, he comes home.

MISS MORGAN. From the City Sanitarium?

MRS. POCCIOTTI. Yes.

MISS MORGAN. Where is he now?

MRS. POCCIOTTI. City Sanitarium.

MISS MORGAN. I see.

MRS. POCCIOTTI. His head is no good. (*With her broom she has fished a lead spoon from under the stove. She stoops, grunting, and places it on the table.*)

MISS MORGAN. Let's see now—your sons?

MRS. POCCIOTTI. Sons? Frank and Tony went off. Was never no good those boys. Tony Chicago, Frank—I think I don't know. I don't know those boys no more where they go, what they do, married or working or nothing those boys I don't know!

MISS MORGAN. Oh! You don't hear from them. What are the others doing?

MRS. POCCIOTTI. Lucio, Silva, the young ones, still are in school.

MISS MORGAN. They're attending grade school?

MRS. POCCIOTTI. Still are in school.

MISS MORGAN. I see. And you have a daughter?

MRS. POCCIOTTI. One girl.

MISS MORGAN. She's also unemployed?

MRS. POCCIOTTI. No, she don't work.

MISS MORGAN. Her name and age, please.

MRS. POCCIOTTI. Name Tina. How old she is? She come right after the last boy, soon as the boys make room comes the girl.

MISS MORGAN. Shall we say that her age is fifteen?

MRS. POCCIOTTI. Fifteen.

MISS MORGAN. I see. I would like to talk to your daughter, Mrs. Pocciotti.

MRS. POCCIOTTI. (*Sweeping with sudden vigor.*) Talk to her?

MISS MORGAN. Yes. Where is she?

MRS. POCCIOTTI. (*Points to closed door.*) In there.

MISS MORGAN. (*Rising.*) May I see her now?

MRS. POCCIOTTI. No. Don't go in. She don't like it.

MISS MORGAN. (*Stiffening.*) She doesn't like it?

MRS. POCCIOTTI. No.

MISS MORGAN. Why not? Is your daughter sick?

MRS. POCCIOTTI. Wharsamatter with her, I dunno. She don't want nobody to go in the room with her, and she don't want the light turned on. She wants it to be always dark.

MISS MORGAN. Dark? Always dark? Really? What do you mean?

MRS. POCCIOTTI. (*With confused gesture.*) Dark!

MISS MORGAN. Will you try to be more co-operative in your answers to questions?

MRS. POCCIOTTI. What?

MISS MORGAN. (*Excitedly.*) Is anything wrong with this girl?

MRS. POCCIOTTI. Wrong? No—I dunno.

MISS MORGAN. And yet you say that she confines herself to a dark room and wishes to be left alone?

MRS. POCCIOTTI. Yes.

MISS MORGAN. Well, of course that isn't a perfectly normal condition for a young girl to be in. Do you realize that?

MRS. POCCIOTTI. (*Slowly shaking her head.*) No.

MISS MORGAN. (*Snapping.*) How long has this been going on?

MRS. POCCIOTTI. Long? Long? How long?

MISS MORGAN. Yes.

MRS. POCCIOTTI. Yes, I think maybe God knows . . . (*She touches her cheek as though she had been struck there—then slowly continues sweeping.*)

MISS MORGAN. (*Distinctly stressing each syllable.*) How long has she been in that room? Days? Weeks? Months?—What? Mrs. Pocciotti, it seems necessary to inform you that there is an element of time we go by. Time measured by the clock, by the calendar, by the—time! Time! Do you understand what time means?

MRS. POCCIOTTI. Time?

MISS MORGAN. Yes. Now how long has your daughter been in this condition?

MRS. POCCIOTTI. (*Quietly after a pause.*) Six mon's.

MISS MORGAN. Six months? She's been in there in the dark for that long? Are you sure?

MRS. POCCIOTTI. Six mon's.

MISS MORGAN. How did this start?

MRS. POCCIOTTI. On New Year's, he didn't come over. It started that night. It was first that he didn't come over in a long time so she called up his place and his Mama said he was out and not to call him no more. She said he was going to be married with some German girl in just a few days and they didn't want to be bothered.

MISS MORGAN. He? He? Who is *he*?

MRS. POCCIOTTI. The boy that she went steady with. Name was Max.

MISS MORGAN. And you feel that her disappointment over this boy is what caused her to have this depressed mental state?

MRS. POCCIOTTI. What?

MISS MORGAN. After that she went in the dark room? You think that was how it was started?

MRS. POCCIOTTI. Maybe it was. I dunno. She phoned him from down at the drugstore and then she comes up to the kitchen and heated some water. She said she had pains in her stummick. Bad pains.

MISS MORGAN. Did she?

MRS. POCCIOTTI. I dunno. Maybe she did. Anyhow she went to bed with it and ain't been up from it since. (*Her broom makes timid excursions around* MISS MORGAN'S *chair. The social service worker draws her feet in like a cat avoiding spilled water.*)

MISS MORGAN. You mean that she's been shut up in the room ever since?

MRS. POCCIOTTI. Yes.

MISS MORGAN. Since New Year's, you said? Six months!

MRS. POCCIOTTI. Six mon's.

MISS MORGAN. Doesn't she *ever* come out?

MRS. POCCIOTTI. When she's got to go to the bathroom, then she comes out. But other times she stays in.

MISS MORGAN. What does she do in there?

MRS. POCCIOTTI. I dunno. She just lays in there in the dark. Sometimes she makes noise.

MISS MORGAN. Noise?

MRS. POCCIOTTI. Crying and calling bad names and knocking her hands on the wall. Upstairs they complain sometimes. But mostly she don't say nothing. Just lays in there on the bed.

MISS MORGAN. How about eating? Does she take regular meals?

MRS. POCCIOTTI. She eats what he brings her.

MISS MORGAN. He? Who do you mean, Mrs. Pocciotti?

MRS. POCCIOTTI. Max.

MISS MORGAN. Max?

MRS. POCCIOTTI. The boy that she went steady with.

MISS MORGAN. Mrs. Pocciotti, you don't mean to say that that boy is still permitted to see your daughter?

MRS. POCCIOTTI. Yes.

MISS MORGAN. But you said he got married?

MRS. POCCIOTTI. Yes. To that German girl. His folks was against our religion.

MISS MORGAN. And still he comes here? Married? He sees your daughter?

MRS. POCCIOTTI. She won't let nobody else in except Max.

MISS MORGAN. Lets him? In the room? With the girl?

MRS. POCCIOTTI. Yes.

MISS MORGAN. She knows that he's married? Of course she knows about that?

MRS. POCCIOTTI. How does she know what I know? I dunno. I can't tell you what I dunno.

MISS MORGAN. He goes in the girl's room. What do they talk about?

MRS. POCCIOTTI. Talk about? Nothing.

MISS MORGAN. They talk about—nothing?

MRS. POCCIOTTI. Nothing.

MISS MORGAN. You mean they don't talk?

MRS. POCCIOTTI. Excuse while I take off the table. (*Removes a cloth from table.*)

MISS MORGAN. Then what—what—what do they *do* in there, Mrs. Pocciotti?

MRS. POCCIOTTI. I dunno. It's dark. I can't tell. He goes in and stays and comes out.

MISS MORGAN. Do I understand you correctly? The man, married, your daughter in such a condition, still you allow him to visit the girl in the dark, you leave them alone in there, you don't know what they're doing?

MRS. POCCIOTTI. Yes. She likes him to go in there. It makes her be not so much noise. You know. When he don't come around a few days, she takes on something awful. Hollering, screaming, never you heard such bad names! Upstairs—complains! When he comes —right away better! Eats what he brings her! That way it helps a lot, too. We don't go so much in the house. Maybe relief she don't come. Max—loaf of bread, cheese, pickle, maybe some coffee even. It helps. (LUCIO *appears at window on fire-escape.*)

LUCIO. Mama!

MRS. POCCIOTTI. Yes.

LUCIO. Gimme two nickels. I bet Jeeps he couldn't lick me an' he did an' he says he'll beat me up worse if I don't come acrost wit' the money!

MRS. POCCIOTTI. Shut up! (*Jerks thumb at* MISS MORGAN'S *back.* LUCIO *looks startled and clatters downstairs. Shrill cries from below.*)

MISS MORGAN. I suppose you know, Mrs. Pocciotti, that you can be held liable for this?

MRS. POCCIOTTI. What?

MISS MORGAN. How long has it been going on? Between this man and your daughter?

MRS. POCCIOTTI. Max? I think maybe God knows.

MISS MORGAN. Mrs. Pocciotti, I have the feeling that you're deliberately evading my questions! That doesn't improve matters any. Co-operation from you will simplify things a great deal.

MRS. POCCIOTTI. You speak funny things. I don't think. I try, but I don't make it out.

MISS MORGAN. I don't think you try very hard. Now if you concentrate less on that aimless sweeping back and forth with a broom —if you listen to what I ask you—if you try to give sensible answers—things will get on much better.—How long has your daughter and this German boy been going together?

MRS. POCCIOTTI. (*Violently.*) Question, you get me mix up! Question, question! How do I know what's wrong?

MISS MORGAN. Tina! Max! How long did they go out together?

MRS. POCCIOTTI. Since school, since beginning at school!

MISS MORGAN. And after your daughter got sick and shut herself up in the dark, when did the boy start coming in that room with her?

MRS. POCCIOTTI. Maybe five or six mon's.

MISS MORGAN. And you and your husband, Mrs. Pocciotti, neither of you did anything to prevent him from coming?

MRS. POCCIOTTI. My husban' is head is no good. I got work to do. We get along best as we can. What happens is God's will, I guess. What is wrong is wrong, I dunno! Is all I can say.

MISS MORGAN. (*Pause.*) I see. Mrs. Pocciotti, the girl will have to be taken away.

MRS. POCCIOTTI. Take her away? She won't like it.

MISS MORGAN. I'm afraid we can't consult her wishes in the matter. Nor yours, either. You've shown yourself completely incompetent to care for this girl. I think I may say that you have even contributed to her delinquency.

MRS. POCCIOTTI. I don't think she'll want to be going. You don't know Tina. She fights, she kicks something awful.

MISS MORGAN. If she won't go peaceably, she'll have to be removed by force.

MRS. POCCIOTTI. I hope she will go. It's bad for the boys, her laying there naked like that.

MISS MORGAN. What? Lying *naked*?

MRS. POCCIOTTI. Yes. She won't keep the clothes on her. The boys look in through the door and they laugh and they say bad things.

MISS MORGAN. (*In disgust.*) Tch, tch, she'll have to be taken away and held for a long observation. (*She rises.*)

MRS. POCCIOTTI. Better you make it be soon. From the way she is looking.

MISS MORGAN. What do you mean? How has your daughter been looking, Mrs. Pocciotti?

MRS. POCCIOTTI. Like—this. (*Her curved palm moves slowly before her abdomen in a broadly elliptical gesture.*)

MISS MORGAN. Oh! You mean ——? (*She raises her hand to her lips.* MRS. POCCIOTTI *nods slowly—goes on with her sweeping.*)

SLOW CURTAIN

THE CASE OF THE CRUSHED PETUNIAS [1]

A LYRICAL FANTASY

This play is respectfully dedicated to the talent and charm of
Miss Helen Hayes—Key West, February, 1941

CHARACTERS

DOROTHY SIMPLE

POLICE OFFICER

YOUNG MAN

MRS. DULL

SCENE: *The action of the play takes place in the Simple
Notion Shop, owned and operated by* MISS DOROTHY
SIMPLE, *a New England maiden of twenty-six, who is
physically very attractive but has barricaded her house
and her heart behind a double row of petunias.*

*The town is Primanproper, Massachusetts, which lies
within the cultural orbit of Boston.*

The play starts in the early morning. MISS SIMPLE, *very
agitated for some reason, has just opened her little shop.
She stands in the open door in a flood of spring sunlight,
but her face expresses grief and indignation. She is calling to a* POLICE OFFICER *on the corner.*

DOROTHY. Officer?—Officer!
OFFICER. (*Strolling up to her.*) Yes, Miss Simple?
DOROTHY. I wish to report a case of deliberate and malicious
sabotage!
OFFICER. Sabotage of what, Miss Simple?
DOROTHY. Of my petunias!

1 Copyright, 1948, by Tennessee Williams.

22

OFFICER. Well, well, well. Now what do you mean by that?

DOROTHY. Exactly what I said. You can see for yourself. Last night this house was surrounded by a beautiful double row of pink and lavender petunias. Look at them now! When I got up this morning I discovered them in this condition. Every single little petunia deliberately and maliciously crushed under foot!

OFFICER. My goodness! Well, well, well!

DOROTHY. "Well, well, well" is not going to catch the culprit!

OFFICER. What do you want me to do, Miss Simple?

DOROTHY. I want you to apprehend a petuniacidal maniac with a size eleven D foot.

OFFICER. Eleven D?

DOROTHY. Yes. That is the size of the footprints that crushed my petunias. I just now had them measured by a shoe clerk.

OFFICER. That's a pretty large foot, Miss Simple, but lots of men have got large feet.

DOROTHY. Not in Primanproper, Massachusetts. Mr. Knowzit, the shoe clerk, assured me that there isn't a man in town who wears a shoe that size. Of course you realize the danger of allowing this maniac to remain at large. Any man who would crush a sweet petunia is equally capable in my opinion of striking a helpless woman or kicking an innocent child!

OFFICER. I'll do my best, Miss Simple. See yuh later.

DOROTHY. (Curtly.) Yes. Good-bye. (Slams door. She returns behind her notion counter and drums restively with her pale pink-polished nails. The canary cheeps timidly. Then tries an arpeggio. DOROTHY, to canary.) Oh, hush up! (Then contritely.) Excuse me, please. My nerves are all to pieces! (Blows her nose. The doorbell tinkles as a customer enters. He is a young man, shockingly large and aggressive looking in the flower-papered cubicle of the shop.) Gracious, please be careful. You're bumping your head against my chandelier.

YOUNG MAN. (Good-humoredly.) Sorry, Miss Simple. I guess I'd better sit down. (The delicate little chair collapses beneath him.)

DOROTHY. Heaven have mercy upon us! You seem to have a genius for destruction! You've broken that little antique chair to smithereens!

YOUNG MAN. Sorry, Miss Simple.

DOROTHY. I appreciate your sorrow, but that won't mend my chair. —Is there anything I can show you in the way of notions?

YOUNG MAN. I'd like to see that pair of wine-colored socks you have in the window.

DOROTHY. What size socks do you wear?

YOUNG MAN. I keep forgetting. But my shoes are eleven D.

DOROTHY. (Sharply.) What size did you say? Eleven? Eleven D?

YOUNG MAN. That's right, Miss Simple. Eleven D.

DOROTHY. Oh. Your shoes are rather muddy, aren't they?

YOUNG MAN. That's right, Miss Simple, I believe they are.

DOROTHY. Quite muddy. It looks like you might have stepped in a freshly watered flower-bed last night.

YOUNG MAN. Come to think of it, that's what I did.

DOROTHY. I don't suppose you've heard about that horrible case of petunia crushing which occurred last night?

YOUNG MAN. As a matter of fact, I have heard something about it.

DOROTHY. From the policeman on the corner?

YOUNG MAN. No, ma'am. Not from him.

DOROTHY. Who from, then? He's the only man who knows about it except—except—except—the man who *did* it! (*Pause. The canary cheeps inquiringly.*) You—you—*you*—are the man who *did* it!

YOUNG MAN. Yes, Miss Simple. I am the man who did it.

DOROTHY. Don't try to get away!

YOUNG MAN. I won't, Miss Simple.

DOROTHY. Stand right where you are till the officer comes!

YOUNG MAN. You're going to call the officer?

DOROTHY. Yes, I am, I certainly am.—In a minute. First I'd like to ask you *why* you *did* it? Why did you crush my petunias?

YOUNG MAN. Okay. I'll tell you why. First, because you'd barricaded your house—and also your heart—behind that silly little double row of petunias!

DOROTHY. Barricaded? My house—my heart—behind them? That's absurd. I don't know what you mean.

YOUNG MAN. I know. They're apparently such delicate, fragile creatures, these petunias, but they have a terrible resistance.

DOROTHY. Resistance to what, may I ask?

YOUNG MAN. Anything big or important that happens to come by your house. Nothing big or important can ever get by a double row of petunias! That is the reason why you are living alone with your canary and beginning to dislike it.

DOROTHY. Dislike my canary? I love it!

24

YOUNG MAN. Secretly, Miss Simple, you wish the bird-seed would choke it! You dislike it nearly as much as you secretly disliked your petunias.

DOROTHY. Why should I, why should you, why should anybody dislike petunias!

YOUNG MAN. Our animosity and its resultant action is best ex plained by a poem I once composed on the subject of petunias— and similar flora. Would you like to hear it?

DOROTHY. I suppose I should, if it's relevant to the case.

YOUNG MAN. Extremely relevant. It goes like this:

(LIGHT MUSIC.)

> How grimly do petunias look
> on things not listed in the book
>
> For these dear creatures never move
> outside the academic groove.
>
> They mark with sharp and moral eye
> phenomena that pass them by
>
> And classify as good or evil
> mammoth whale or tiny weevil.
>
> They note with consummate disdain
> all that is masculine or plain
>
> They blush down to their tender roots
> when men pass by in working boots
>
> All honest language shocks them so
> they cringe to hear a rooster crow
>
> Of course they say that good clean fun's
> permissible for *every* one
>
> But find that even Blindman's Bluff
> is noisy and extremely rough
>
> AND—
> (*Stage whisper.*)—Not quite innocent enough!

What do you think of it?

DOROTHY. Unfair! Completely unfair!

YOUNG MAN. (*Laughing.*) To organized petunias?

DOROTHY. Yes, and besides, I don't think anyone has the right to impose his opinions in the form of footprints on other people's petunias!

YOUNG MAN. (Removing small package from pocket.) I'm prepared to make complete restitution.

DOROTHY. What with?

YOUNG MAN. With these.

DOROTHY. What are they?

YOUNG MAN. Seeds.

DOROTHY. Seeds of what? Sedition?

YOUNG MAN. No. Wild roses.

DOROTHY. Wild? I couldn't use them!

YOUNG MAN. Why not, Miss Simple?

DOROTHY. Flowers are like human beings. They can't be allowed to grow wild. They have to be ——

YOUNG MAN. Regimented? Ahhh. I see. You're a horticultural fascist!

DOROTHY. (With an indignant gasp.) I ought to call the policeman about those petunias!

YOUNG MAN. Why don't you, then?

DOROTHY. Only because you made an honest confession.

YOUNG MAN. That's not why, Miss Simple.

DOROTHY. No?

YOUNG MAN. The actual reason is that you are fascinated.

DOROTHY. *AM* I? Indeed!

YOUNG MAN. Indeed you are, Miss Simple. In spite of your late unlamented petunias, you're charmed, you're intrigued—you're frightened!

DOROTHY. You're very conceited!

YOUNG MAN. Now, if you please, I'd like to ask you a question.

DOROTHY. You may. But I may not answer.

YOUNG MAN. You will if you can. But you probably won't be able. The question is this: What do you make of it all?

DOROTHY. I don't understand —— All *what?*

YOUNG MAN. The world? The universe? And your position in it? This miraculous accident of being alive! (SOFT MUSIC BACKGROUND.) Has it ever occurred to you how much the living are outnumbered by the dead? Their numerical superiority, Miss Simple, is so tremendous that you couldn't possibly find a ratio with figures vast enough *above* the line, and small enough *below* to represent it.

DOROTHY. You sound like you were trying to sell me something.

YOUNG MAN. I am, I am, just wait!

DOROTHY. I'm not in the market for ——

YOUNG MAN. Please! One minute of your infinitely valuable time!

DOROTHY. All right. One minute.

YOUNG MAN. *Look!*

DOROTHY. At what?

YOUNG MAN. Those little particles of dust in the shaft of April sunlight through that window.

DOROTHY. What about them?

YOUNG MAN. Just think. You might have been one of those instead of what you are. You might have been any one of those infinitesimal particles of dust. Or any one of millions and billions and trillions of other particles of mute, unconscious matter. Never capable of asking any questions. Never capable of giving any answers. Never capable of doing, thinking, feeling anything at all! But instead, dear lady, by the rarest and most improbable of accidents, you happened to be what you are. Miss Dorothy Simple from Boston! Beautiful. Human. Alive. Capable of thought and feeling and action. Now here comes the vital part of my question. What are you going to *do* about it, Miss Simple?

DOROTHY. (*Who is somewhat moved, in spite of her crushed petunias.*) Well, goodness—gracious—sakes alive! I thought you came in here to buy some socks?

YOUNG MAN. Yes, but I've got to sell *you* something first.

DOROTHY. Sell me what?

YOUNG MAN. A wonderful bill of goods.

DOROTHY. I'll have to see it before I sign the order.

YOUNG MAN. That's impossible. I can't display my samples in this shoppe.

DOROTHY. Why not?

YOUNG MAN. They're much too precious. You have to make an appointment.

DOROTHY. (*Retreating.*) Sorry. But I do all my business in here.

YOUNG MAN. Too bad for you.—In fact, too bad for us both. Maybe you'll change your mind?

DOROTHY. I don't think so.

YOUNG MAN. Anyway, here's my card.

DOROTHY. (*Reading it, bewildered.*)—LIFE—INCORPORATED. (*Looks up slowly.*)

YOUNG MAN. Yes. I represent that line.

DOROTHY. I see. You're a magazine salesman?

YOUNG MAN. No. It isn't printed matter.

DOROTHY. But it's matter, though?

YOUNG MAN. Oh, yes, and it's matter of tremendous importance, too. But it's neglected by people. Because of their ignorance they've been buying cheap substitute products. And lately a rival concern has sprung up outside the country. This firm is known as DEATH, UNLIMITED. Their product comes in a package labelled WAR. They're crowding us out with new aggressive methods of promotion. And one of their biggest sales-points is EXCITEMENT. Why does it work so well? Because you little people surround your houses and also your hearts with rows of tiresome, trivial little things like petunias! If we could substitute wild roses there wouldn't be wars! No, there'd be excitement enough in the world *without* having wars! That's why we've started this petunia-crushing campaign, Miss Simple. Life, Incorporated, has come to the realization that we have to use the same aggressive methods of promotion used by DEATH, UNLIMITED over there! We've got to show people that the malignantly trivial little petunias of the world can be eliminated more cleanly, permanently and completely by LIFE, INCORPORATED than by DEATH, UNLIMITED! Now what do you say, Miss Simple? Won't you try our product?

DOROTHY. (*Nervously.*) Well, you see it's like this—I do all my buying in Boston and ——

YOUNG MAN. What do you buy in Boston?

DOROTHY. You can see for yourself. Look over the stock.

YOUNG MAN. (*Examining the shelves.*) Thimbles—threads—ladies' needle-work—white gloves ——

DOROTHY. Notions. Odds and ends.

YOUNG MAN. Odds and ends—of existence?

DOROTHY. Yes, that's it exactly.

YOUNG MAN. What do you do after hours?

DOROTHY. I carry on a lot of correspondence.

YOUNG MAN. Who with?

DOROTHY. With wholesale firms in Boston.

YOUNG MAN. How do you sign your letters?

DOROTHY. "Sincerely." "As ever." "Very truly yours."

YOUNG MAN. But never with love?

DOROTHY. Love? To firms in Boston?

YOUNG MAN. I guess not. I think you ought to enlarge your correspondence. I'll tell you what I'll do. I'll meet you tonight on Highway No. 77!

DOROTHY. Oh, no! I have my correspondence!

YOUNG MAN. Delay your correspondence. Meet me there. We'll have a couple of beers at the Starlight Casino.

DOROTHY. (*With frantic evasion.*) But I don't drink!

YOUNG MAN. Then *eat.* Swiss cheese on rye. It doesn't matter. Afterwards I'll take you for a ride in an open car.

DOROTHY. Where to?

YOUNG MAN. To Cypress Hill.

DOROTHY. Why, that's the cemetery.

YOUNG MAN. Yes, I know.

DOROTHY. Why there?

YOUNG MAN. Because dead people give the best advice.

DOROTHY. Advice on what?

YOUNG MAN. The problems of the living.

DOROTHY. What advice do they give?

YOUNG MAN. Just one word: *Live!*

DOROTHY. Live?

YOUNG MAN. Yes, live, live, live! It's all they know, it's the only word left in their vocabulary!

DOROTHY. I don't see how ——?

YOUNG MAN. I'll tell you how. There's one thing in Death's favor. It's a wonderful process of simplification. It rids the heart of all inconsequentials. For instance, it goes through the dictionary with an absolutely merciless blue pencil. Finally all that you've got left's one page—and on that page one word!

DOROTHY. The word you hear at night on Cypress Hill?

YOUNG MAN. The word you hear at night on Cypress Hill!

DOROTHY. Ohhh. Oh, oh!

YOUNG MAN. But no one hears it till they deal with *me.* I have a secret patented device that makes it audible to them. Something never processed by Du Pont. But none the less a marvelous inven tion. It's absolutely weightless and transparent. It fits insic ` ` ear. Your friends won't even know you have it on. But this I antee: you'll hear that word, that sound much like the long, sweet sound of leaves in motion!

DOROTHY. Leaves?

YOUNG MAN. Yes, willow leaves or leaves of cypresses or leaves of wind-blown grass! And afterwards you'll never be the same. No, you'll be changed forever!

DOROTHY. In what way?

YOUNG MAN. You'll live, live, *live!*—And not behind petunias. How about it, Miss Simple? Dorothy? Is it a date? Tonight at half-past eight on No. 77?

DOROTHY. Whereabouts on Highway No. 77?

YOUNG MAN. By the wild plum-tree—at the broken place in the long stone wall—where roots have cleft the rocks and made them crumble.

DOROTHY. It sounds so far. It sounds—unicivilized.

YOUNG MAN. It is uncivilized, but it isn't far.

DOROTHY. How would I get out there? What means of transportation?

YOUNG MAN. Borrow your kid brother's bike.

DOROTHY. Tonight's Scout meeting night; he wouldn't let me.

YOUNG MAN. Then walk, it wouldn't kill you!

DOROTHY. How do you know? It might. I come from Boston.

YOUNG MAN. Listen, lady. Boston's a state of mind that you'll grow out of.

DOROTHY. Not without some insulin shock treatments.

YOUNG MAN. Stop evading! Will you or will you not?

DOROTHY. I've got so much to do. I have to return some books to the public library.

YOUNG MAN. Just one more time—will you or will you not?

DOROTHY. I can't give definite answers—I'm from Boston!

YOUNG MAN. Just one more mention of Boston's apt to be fatal! Well, Miss Simple? I can't wait forever!

DOROTHY. I guess I—might.

YOUNG MAN. You guess you *might?*

DOROTHY. I mean I guess I will.

YOUNG MAN. You *guess* you will?

DOROTHY. I mean I will—I *will!*

YOUNG MAN. That's better.—So long, Dorothy. (*He grins and goes out, slamming door.*)

DOROTHY. Good-bye. (*She stares dreamily into space for a moment.* MRS. DULL *comes in.*)

MRS. DULL. (*Sharply.*) Miss Simple!

DOROTHY. Oh! Excuse me. What do you want?

MRS. DULL. I want a pair of wine-colored socks for my husband.

DOROTHY. I'm terribly sorry but the only pair in stock have been reserved.

MRS. DULL. Reserved for whom, Miss Simple?

DOROTHY. A gentleman who represents this line. (*Showing card.*)

MRS. DULL. Life, Incorporated? Huh, I never heard of it.

DOROTHY. Neither had I before. But now I have. And tomorrow the store will be closed for extensive alterations.

MRS. DULL. Alterations of what kind, Miss Simple?

DOROTHY. I'm going to knock out all four walls.

MRS. DULL. Knock out—what ——? Incredible!

DOROTHY. Yes, to accommodate some brand-new merchandise. Things I never kept in stock before.

MRS. DULL. What kind of things? Things in bottles, Miss Simple, or things in boxes?

DOROTHY. Neither one nor the other, Mrs. Dull.

MRS. DULL. But everything comes in bottles or in boxes.

DOROTHY. Everything but Life, Incorporated.

MRS. DULL. What does it come in, then?

DOROTHY. I'm not sure yet. But I suspect it's something unconfined, something wild and open as the sky is!—Also I'm going to change the name of the store. It isn't going to be SIMPLE NOTIONS any more, it's going to be TREMENDOUS INSPIRATIONS!

MRS. DULL. Gracious! In that case you'll certainly lose my custom.

DOROTHY. I rather expected to.

MRS. DULL. And you're not sorry?

DOROTHY. Not the least bit sorry. I think I caught a slight skin rash from dealing with your silver. Also you sniff too much. You ought to blow your nose. Or better still, you ought to trim it down. I've often wondered how you get your nose through traffic. (MRS. DULL *gasps, looks desperately about her, rushes out.*) You forgot your groceries, Mrs. Dull! (*Heaves them out the door. Loud impact, sharp outcry. Music up.*) Officer?—Officer!

OFFICER. Did you say size eleven D, Miss Simple?

DOROTHY. Never mind that now, that's all been settled.

OFFICER. Amicably? Out of court, you mean?

DOROTHY. Amicably and out of court. The saboteur has made full restitution and the case is dropped. Now what I want to ask of you is this: how do I get out to No. 77?

OFFICER. Highway No. 77? That road's abandoned.

DOROTHY. Not by me. Where is it?

OFFICER. It's in an awful condition, it's overgrown by brambles!

DOROTHY. I don't care! Where is it?

OFFICER. They say the rain has loosened half the stones. Also the wind has taken liberties with it. The moon at night makes such confusing shadows people lose their way, go dangerous places, do outrageous things!

DOROTHY. Things such as what?

OFFICER. Oh—senseless acrobatics, cart-wheels in mid-air, unheard of songs they sing, distil the midnight vapors into wine—do pagan dances!

DOROTHY. Marvelous! How do I get there?

OFFICER. I warn you, Miss Simple, once you go that way you can't come back to Primanproper, Massachusetts!

DOROTHY. Who wants to come back here? Not I! Never was anyone a more willing candidate for expatriation than I am tonight! All I want to know is where it is —— Is it north, south, or east or west of town?

OFFICER. That's just it, ma'am. It's in all four directions.

DOROTHY. Then I don't suppose that I could possibly miss it.

OFFICER. Hardly possibly, if you want to find it. Is that all?

DOROTHY. Yes, sir, that's all.—Thanks very much.—Good-bye! (MUSIC UP. DOROTHY *softly*.) Good-bye forever!

THE LONG STAY CUT SHORT,
OR,
THE UNSATISFACTORY SUPPER [1]

THREE CHARACTERS

BABY DOLL

ARCHIE LEE

AUNT ROSE

THE CURTAIN RISES *on the porch and side yard of a shot-*
gun cottage in Blue Mountain, Mississippi. The frame
house is faded and has a greenish-gray cast with dark
streaks from the roof, and there are irregularities in the
lines of the building. Behind it the dusky cyclorama is
stained with the rose of sunset, which is stormy-looking,
and the wind has a cat-like whine.

Upstage from the porch, in the center of the side yard,
is a very large rose-bush, the beauty of which is some-
how sinister-looking.

A Prokofief sort of music introduces the scene and sets a
mood of grotesque lyricism.

The screen door opens with a snarl of rusty springs and
latches: this stops the music.

MRS. "BABY DOLL" BOWMAN *appears. She is a large and*
indolent woman, but her amplitude is not benign, her
stupidity is not comfortable. There is a suggestion of
Egypt in the arrangement of her glossy black hair and
the purple linen dress and heavy brass jewelry that she
is wearing.

ARCHIE LEE BOWMAN *comes out and sucks at his teeth.*
He is a large man with an unhealthy chalk-white face
and slack figure.

(*The evenly cadenced lines of the dialogue between* BABY
DOLL *and* ARCHIE LEE *may be given a singsong reading,*
somewhat like a grotesque choral incantation, and pas-
sages may be divided as strophe and antistrophe by BABY
DOLL'S *movements back and forth on the porch.*)

ARCHIE LEE. The old lady used to could set a right fair table, but
not any more. The food has fallen off bad around here lately.
BABY DOLL. You're right about that, Archie Lee. I can't argue with
you.
ARCHIE LEE. A good mess of greens is a satisfactory meal if it's
cooked with salt-pork an' left on th' stove till it's tender, but
thrown in a platter ha'f cooked an' unflavored, it ain't even fit for
hog-slops.
BABY DOLL. It's hard t' spoil greens but the old lady sure did spoil
'em.
ARCHIE LEE. How did she manage t' do it?
BABY DOLL. (*Slowly and contemptuously.*) Well, she had 'em on
th' stove for about an hour. Said she thought they wuh boilin'. I
went in the kitchen. The stove was stone-cold. The silly old thing
had forgotten to build a fire in it. So I called her back. I said,
"Aunt Rose, I think I understand why the greens aren't boilin'."
"Why aren't they boilin'?" she says. Well, I told her, "it might
have something to do with the fack that the stove issen lighted!"
ARCHIE LEE. What did she say about that?
BABY DOLL. Juss threw back her head an' cackled. "Why, I thought
my stove was lighted," she said. "I thought my greens wuh boilin'."
Everything is *my*. My stove, my greens, my kitchen. She has taken
possession of everything on the place.
ARCHIE LEE. She's getting delusions of grandeur. (*A high, thin*
laugh is heard inside.) Why does she cackle that way?
BABY DOLL. How should I know why she cackles! I guess it's sup-
posed to show that she's in a good humor.
ARCHIE LEE. A thing like that can become awf'ly aggravating.
BABY DOLL. It gets on my nerves so bad I could haul off and
scream. And obstinate! She's just as obstinate as a mule.

34

ARCHIE LEE. A person can be obstinate and still cook greens.

BABY DOLL. Not if they're so obstinate they won't even look in a stove t' see if it's lighted.

ARCHIE LEE. Why don't you keep the old lady out of the kitchen?

BABY DOLL. You get me a nigger and I'll keep her out of the kitchen. (*The screen door creaks open and* AUNT ROSE *comes out on the porch. She is breathless with the exertion of moving from the kitchen, and clings to a porch column while she is catching her breath. She is the type of old lady, about eighty-five years old, that resembles a delicate white-headed monkey. She has on a dress of gray calico which has become too large for her shrunken figure. She has a continual fluttering in her chest which makes her laugh in a witless manner. Neither of the pair on the porch pays any apparent attention to her, though she nods and smiles brightly at each.*)

AUNT ROSE. I brought out m' scissors. Tomorrow is Sunday an' I can't stand for my house to be without flowers on Sunday. Besides if we don't cut the roses the wind'll just blow them away.

BABY DOLL. (*Yawns ostentatiously.* ARCHIE LEE *sucks loudly at his teeth.* BABY DOLL, *venting her irritation.*) Will you quit suckin' your teeth?

ARCHIE LEE. I got something stuck in my teeth an' I can't remove it.

BABY DOLL. There's such a thing as a tooth-pick made for that purpose.

ARCHIE LEE. I told you at breakfast we didn't have any tooth-picks. I told you the same thing at lunch and the same thing at supper. Does it have to appear in the paper for you to believe it?

BABY DOLL. There's other things with a point besides a tooth-pick.

AUNT ROSE. (*Excitedly.*) Archie Lee, Son! (*She produces a spool of thread from her bulging skirt-pocket.*) You bite off a piece of this thread and run it between your teeth and if that don't dislodge a morsel nothing else will!

ARCHIE LEE. (*Slamming his feet from porch-rail to floor.*) Now listen, you all, I want you both to get this. If I want to suck at my teeth, I'm going to suck at my teeth!

AUNT ROSE. That's right, Archie Lee, you go on and suck at your teeth as much as you want to. (BABY DOLL *grunts disgustedly.* ARCHIE LEE *throws his feet back on the rail and continues sucking loudly at his teeth.* AUNT ROSE, *hesitantly.*) Archie Lee, son, you weren't satisfied with your supper. I noticed you left a lot of greens on your plate.

ARCHIE LEE. I'm not strong on greens.

AUNT ROSE. I'm surprised to hear you say that.

ARCHIE LEE. I don't see why you should be. As far as I know I never declared any terrible fondness for greens in your presence, Aunt Rose.

AUNT ROSE. Well, somebody did.

ARCHIE LEE. Somebody probably did sometime and somewhere but that don't mean it was me.

AUNT ROSE. (*With a nervous laugh.*) Baby Doll, who is it dotes on greens so much?

BABY DOLL. (*Wearily.*) I don't know who dotes on greens, Aunt Rose.

AUNT ROSE. All these likes and dislikes, it's hard to keep straight in your head. But Archie Lee's easy t' cook for, yes, he is, easy t' cook for! Jim's a complainer, oh, my, what a complainer. And Susie's household! What complainers! Every living one of them's a complainer! They're such complainers I die of nervous prostration when I'm cooking for them. But Archie Lee, here, he takes whatever you give him an' seems to love ev'ry bite of it! (*She touches his head.*) Bless you, honey, for being so easy t' cook for! (ARCHIE LEE *picks up his chair and moves it roughly away from* AUNT ROSE. *She laughs nervously and digs in her capacious pocket for the scissors.*) Now I'm goin' down there an' clip a few roses befo' th' wind blows 'em away 'cause I can't stand my house to be without flowers on Sunday. An' soon as I've finished with that, I'm goin' back in my kitchen an' light up my stove an' cook you some eggs Birmingham. I won't have my men-folks unsatisfied with their supper. Won't have it, I won't stand for it! (*She gets to the bottom of the steps and pauses for breath.*)

ARCHIE LEE. What is eggs Birmingham?

AUNT ROSE. Why, eggs Birmingham was Baby Doll's daddy's pet dish.

ARCHIE LEE. That don't answer my question.

AUNT ROSE. (*As though confiding a secret.*) I'll tell you how to prepare them.

ARCHIE LEE. I don't care how you prepare them, I just want to know what they are.

AUNT ROSE. (*Reasonably.*) Well, Son, I can't say what they are without telling how to prepare them. You cut some bread-slices and take the centers out of them. You put the bread-slices in a skillet with butter. Then into each cut-out center you drop one egg and on top of the eggs you put the cut-out centers.

ARCHIE LEE. (*Sarcastically.*) Do you build a fire in th' stove?

BABY DOLL. No, you forget to do that. That's why they call them eggs Birmingham, I suppose. (*She laughs at her wit.*)

AUNT ROSE. (*Vivaciously.*) That's what they call them, they call them eggs Birmingham and Baby Doll's daddy was just insane about them. When Baby Doll's daddy was not satisfied with his supper, he'd call for eggs Birmingham and would stomp his feet on the floor until I'd fixed 'em! (*This recollection seems to amuse her so that she nearly falls over.*) He'd stomp his feet on th' floor!—until I'd fixed 'em. . . . (*Her laughter dies out and she wanders away from the porch, examining the scissors.*)

BABY DOLL. That old woman is going out of her mind.

ARCHIE LEE. How long is she been with us?

BABY DOLL. She come in October.

ARCHIE LEE. No, it was August. She pulled in here last August.

BABY DOLL. Was it in August? Yes, it was, it was August.

ARCHIE LEE. Why don't she go an' cackle at Susie's awhile?

BABY DOLL. Susie don't have a bed for her.

ARCHIE LEE. Then how about Jim?

BABY DOLL. She was at Jim's direckly before she come here and Jim's wife said she stole from her and that's why she left.

ARCHIE LEE. I don't believe she stole from her. Do you believe she stole from her?

BABY DOLL. I don't believe she stole from her. I think it was just an excuse to get rid of her. (AUNT ROSE *has arrived at the rose-bush. The wind comes up and nearly blows her off her feet. She staggers around and laughs at her precarious balance.*)

AUNT ROSE. Oh, my gracious! Ha-ha! Oh! Ha-ha-ha!

BABY DOLL. Why, every time I lay my pocket-book down, the silly old thing picks it up and comes creeping in to me with it, and says, "Count the change."

ARCHIE LEE. What does she do that for?

BABY DOLL. She's afraid I'll accuse her of stealing like Jim's wife did.

AUNT ROSE. (*Singing to herself as she creeps around the rose-bush.*)

Rock of Ages, cleft for me,
Let me hide myself in thee!

ARCHIE LEE. Your buck-toothed cousin named Bunny, didn't he hit on a new way of using oil-waste?

BABY DOLL. He did an' he didn't.

ARCHIE LEE. That statement don't make sense.

BABY DOLL. Well, you know Bunny. He hits on something and ropes in a few stockholders and then it blows up and the stockholders all go to court. And also he says that his wife's got female trouble.

ARCHIE LEE. They've all got something because they're not mental giants but they've got enough sense to know the old lady is going to break down pretty soon and none of 'em wants it to be while she's on their hands.

BABY DOLL. That is about the size of it.

ARCHIE LEE. And I'm stuck with her?

BABY DOLL. Don't holler.

ARCHIE LEE. I'm nominated the goat!

BABY DOLL. Don't holler, don't holler! (AUNT ROSE *sings faintly by rose-bush.*)

ARCHIE LEE. Then pass the old lady on to one of them others.

BABY DOLL. Which one, Archie Lee?

ARCHIE LEE. Eeny-meeny-miney-mo.—Mo gets her.

BABY DOLL. Which is "Mo"?

ARCHIE LEE. Not me! (*Moving slowly and cautiously around the rose-bush with her scissors,* AUNT ROSE *sings to herself. Intersperses lines of the hymn with dialogue on porch. A blue dusk is gathering in the yard but a pool of clear light remains upon the rose-bush.* ARCHIE LEE, *with religious awe.*) Some of them get these lingering types of diseases and have to be given morphine, and they tell me that morphine is just as high as a cat's back.

BABY DOLL. Some of them hang on forever, taking morphine.

ARCHIE LEE. And quantities of it!

BABY DOLL. Yes, they take quantities of it!

ARCHIE LEE. Suppose the old lady broke a hip-bone or something, something that called for morphine!

BABY DOLL. The rest of the folks would have to pitch in and help us.

ARCHIE LEE. Try and extract a dime from your brother Jim! Or

Susie or Tom or Bunny! They're all tight as drums, they squeeze ev'ry nickel until th' buffalo bleeds!

BABY DOLL. They don't have much and what they have they hold onto.

ARCHIE LEE. Well, if she does, if she breaks down an' dies on us here, I'm giving you fair warning —— (*Lurches heavily to his feet and spits over edge of porch.*) I'll have her burned up and her ashes put in an old Coca-cola bottle —— (*Flops down again.*) Unless your folks kick in with the price of a coffin! (AUNT ROSE *has clipped a few roses. Now she wanders toward the front of the cottage with them.*) Here she comes back. Now tell her.

BABY DOLL. Tell her what?

ARCHIE LEE. That she's out-stayed her welcome.

AUNT ROSE. (*Still at some distance.*) I want you children to look.

ARCHIE LEE. You going to tell her?

AUNT ROSE. I want you children to look at these poems of nature!

ARCHIE LEE. Or do I have to tell her?

BABY DOLL. You hush up and I'll tell her.

ARCHIE LEE. Then tell her right now, and no more pussy-footing.

AUNT ROSE. (*Now close to the porch.*) Look at them, look at them, children, they're poems of nature! (*But the "Children" stare unresponsively, not at the flowers but at* AUNT ROSE'S *face with its extravagant brightness. She laughs uncertainly and turns to* ARCHIE LEE *for a more direct appeal.*) Archie Lee, aren't they, aren't they just poems of nature? (*He grunts and gets up, and as he passes* BABY DOLL'S *chair he gives it a kick to remind her.* BABY DOLL *clears her throat.*)

BABY DOLL. (*Uneasily.*) Yes, they are poems of nature, Aunt Rose, there is no doubt about it, they are. And, Aunt Rose—while we are talking—step over here for a minute so I can speak to you. (AUNT ROSE *had started away from the porch, as if with a premonition of danger. She stops, her back to the porch, and the fear is visible in her face. It is a familiar fear, one that is graven into her very bones, but which she has never become inured to.*)

AUNT ROSE. What is it, honey? (*She turns around slowly.*) I know you children are feeling upset about something. It don't take a Gypsy with cards to figure that out. You an' Archie Lee both are upset about something. I think you were both unsatisfied with your supper. Isn't that it, Baby Doll? The greens didn't boil long enough. Don't you think I know that? (*She looks from* BABY DOLL'S *face* to ARCHIE LEE'S *back with a hesitant laugh.*) I played a fool trick with my stove, I thought it was lighted and all that time it was . . .

BABY DOLL. Aunt Rose, won't you set down so we can talk com· fortably?

AUNT ROSE. (*With a note of hysteria.*) I don't want to set down, I don't want to set down, I can talk on my feet! I tell you, getting up an' down is more trouble than it's worth! Now what is it, honey? As soon as I've put these in water, I'm going to light up my stove an' cook you two children some Eggs Birmingham. Archie Lee, Son, you hear that?

ARCHIE LEE. (*Roughly, his back still turned.*) I don't want Eggs Birmingham.

BABY DOLL. He don't want Eggs Birmingham and neither do I. But while we are talking, Aunt Rose—well—Archie Lee's wondered and I've been wondering, too . . .

AUNT ROSE. About what, Baby Doll?

BABY DOLL. Well, as to whether or not you've—made any plans.

AUNT ROSE. Plans?

BABY DOLL. Yes, plans.

AUNT ROSE. What kind of plans, Baby Doll?

BABY DOLL. Why, plans for the future, Aunt Rose.

AUNT ROSE. Oh! Future! No—no, when an old maid gets to be nearly a hundred years old, the future don't seem to require much planning for, honey. Many's a time I've wondered but I've never doubted. . . . (*Her voice dies out and there is a strain of music as she faces away from the porch.*) I'm not forgotten by Jesus! No, my Sweet Savior has not forgotten about me! The time isn't known to me or to you, Baby Doll, but it's known by Him and when it comes He will call me. A wind'll come down and lift me an' take me away! The way that it will the roses when they're like I am. . . . (*The music dies out and she turns back to the tribunal on the front porch.*)

BABY DOLL. (*Clearing her throat again.*) That's all very well, Aunt Rose, to trust in Jesus, but we've got to remember that Jesus only helps those that—well—help themselves!

AUNT ROSE. Oh, I know that, Baby Doll! (*She laughs.*) Why, I learned that in my cradle, I reckon I must have learned that before I was born. Now when have I ever been helpless? I could count my sick days, the days that I haven't been up and around, on my fingers! My Sweet Savior has kept me healthy an' active, active an'

40

healthy, yes, I do pride myself on it, my age hasn't made me a burden! And when the time comes that I have to lean on His shoulder, I —— (ARCHIE LEE *turns about roughly.*)

ARCHIE LEE. All this talk about Jesus an' greens didn't boil an' so forth has got nothing at all to do with the situation! Now look here, Aunt Rose ——

BABY DOLL. (*Getting up.*) Archie Lee, will you hold your tongue for a minute?

ARCHIE LEE. Then you talk up! And plain! What's there to be so pussy-footing about?

BABY DOLL. There's ways and there's ways of talking anything over!

ARCHIE LEE. Well, talk it over and get off the subject of Jesus! There's Susie, there's Jim, there's Tom and Jane and there's Bunny! And if none of them suits her, there's homes in the county will take her! Just let her decide on which one she is ready to visit. First thing in the morning I'll pile her things in the car and drive her out to whichever one's she's decided! Now ain't that a simple procedure compared to all of this pussy-footing around? Aunt Rose has got sense. She's counted the rooms in this house! She knows that I'm nervous, she knows that I've got work to do and a workingman's got to be fed! And his house is his house and he wants it the way that he wants it! Well, Jesus Almighty, if that's not a plain, fair and square way of settling the matter, I'll wash my hands clean and leave you two women to talk it over yourselves! Yes, I'll —be God damned if ——! (*He rushes in and slams the screen door. There is a long pause in which* BABY DOLL *looks uncomfortably at nothing, and* AUNT ROSE *stares at the screen door.*)

AUNT ROSE. (*Finally.*) I thought you children were satisfied with my cooking. (*A blue dusk has gathered in the yard.* AUNT ROSE *moves away from the porch and there is a strain of music. The music is drowned out by the cat-like whine of the wind turning suddenly angry.* BABY DOLL *gets up from her wicker chair.*)

BABY DOLL. Archie Lee, Archie Lee, you help me in with these chairs before they blow over! (*She drags her chair to the screen door.*) It looks and sounds like a twister! Hold that screen open for me! Pull in that chair! Now this one! We better get down in the cellar! (*As an after-thought.*) Aunt Rose, come in here so we can shut this door! (AUNT ROSE *shakes her head slightly. Then she looks toward the sky, above and beyond the proscenium, where*

something portentous is forming. BABY DOLL *back in the house.)*
Call Aunt Rose in!

ARCHIE LEE. *(Near the door.)* The stubborn old thing won't budge.
*(The door slams shut. The whine of the angry cat turns into a
distant roar and the roar approaches. But* AUNT ROSE *remains in the
yard, her face still somberly but quietly thoughtful. The loose gray
calico of her dress begins to whip and tug at the skeleton lines of
her figure. She looks wonderingly at the sky, then back at the house
beginning to shrink into darkness, then back at the sky from which
the darkness is coming, at each with the same unflinching but
troubled expression. Nieces and nephews and cousins, like pages
of an album, are rapidly turned through her mind, some of them
loved as children but none of them really her children and all of
them curiously unneedful of the devotion that she had offered so
freely, as if she had always carried an armful of roses that no one
had ever offered a vase to receive. The flimsy gray scarf is whipped
away from her shoulders. She makes an awkward gesture and
sinks to her knees. Her arms let go of the roses. She reaches
vaguely after them. One or two she catches. The rest blow away.
She struggles back to her feet. The blue dusk deepens to purple
and the purple to black and the roar comes on with the force of a
locomotive as* AUNT ROSE'S *figure is still pushed toward the rose-
bush.)*

THE CURTAIN FALLS

42

TEN BLOCKS ON THE CAMINO REAL [1][2]

A FANTASY

CHARACTERS

KILROY........................25, a vagrant, former boxer
MARGUERITE GAUTIER
JACQUES CASANOVA
BARON DE CHARLUS
MR. GUTMAN.................Proprietor of the Siete Mares
THE GYPSY
HER DAUGHTER, ESMERALDA
DON QUIXOTE
SANCHO PANZA
LA MADRECITA DE LAS SOLEDADAS (*Flower vendor*)
AN OFFICER
A PEASANT
A SINGER
A GUITAR PLAYER
A CHORUS OF ABOUT TEN DANCERS
TWO STREET-CLEANERS

THE PLACE is ostensibly a small tropical port of the Americas.
The audience faces a little plaza. It should have grace and
mystery and sadness: that peculiar dreamlike feeling that ema-
nates from such squares in Mexico and from the popular songs of
that country. In full light it suggests a drawing in pastels, with the
chalky white of adobe walls and the delicate tints of rain-washed
and sun-bleached posters. The plaza is contained by three street-
façades and in its center is a shallow dried-up fountain. Along the
back of plaza, parallel to the proscenium, is *El Camino Real* designated by a street-sign. On this is the central playing area, The
Gypsy's Establishment, the facing wall of which is a transparency
that is lifted for an interior scene. On this transparency painted, a

---

[1] Use Anglicized pronunciation: ka′-mino re′-al.
[2] Copyright, 1948, by Tennessee Williams.

sign: HOY! NOCHE DE FIESTA! THE MOON WILL RE-
STORE THE VIRGINITY OF MY DAUGHTER!! (this being in
Spanish). The entrance to the establishment is on the narrow cob-
bled alley that issues upstage from the (stage) left side of the
plaza. This alley is steep as a flight of stairs (such alleys are
common in mountain villages of Mexico) and it climbs to a
crumbling yellow arch level with the roof of the Gypsy's. Perched
on the arch is a carrion bird; beyond it, and over the roofs of the
village, is a vista of country like a landscape on the moon which
extends to a range of blue and white mountains. The alley has a
sign that says: THIS WAY OUT.

On the right is the *Siete Mares* hotel façade and portico and the
entrance to its cantina. This façade is designed for first class
tourist-trade. The walls are turquoise and decorated with devices
of the sea, such as star-fish and conch-shells and leaping dolphins.
Before the hotel is a small round table and two chairs, both of
graceful white iron-work. On the opposite side of the plaza is the
door and window of a pawn-shop, frankly called THE LOAN
SHARK. Over it three yellow balls.

As the curtain rises there are stationary figures about the plaza.
These figures will be variously used as vendors, dancers and chorus
of the "Laboratory" scene. A group of ten dancers would suffice
for all chorus uses. They are crouching, leaning and lying about
the plaza in their dust-colored rags. They have a look of immense
torpor as if they were stunned or drugged by the great ball of
fire that rolls gradually over the nameless town and country. One
of the street-figures is distinct from the others. She is an ancient
woman who wears a snow-white rebozo and who is vending those
glittering and gaudy flowers made of tin that are used at peasant
funerals in the Latin Americas. Her voice is softer and more
musical than the others, and her face remains hidden by the blanket
until the "Laboratory" scene when she becomes La Madrecita de
las Soledadas. Seated by fountain or base of alley.

Also distinct from the others is a guitar player whose instru-
ment is blue: he is dressed as a Mexican street-musician, though
he may wear a domino to indicate he is somewhat outside the
play, being a sort of master of ceremonies. The guitar and singing
may be used at more points than are indicated in the script: the
**same is true of dancing; though it should not impede a lively
progress of scenes. Lightness and quickness should be the keynote**

of the production: that is, in physical movement, except where otherwise indicated.

Only the guitar player stands erect as the curtain rises. He strikes a sombre chord.

BLOCK I

> *At this signal a cry is heard. A FIGURE in rags, skin blackened by the sun, tumbles crazily through the arch and down the steep alley to the fountain. There he throws himself on his stomach and thrusts both hands into the dried basin. He staggers to his feet and gives a despairing cry.*

FIGURE. *La Fuente esta seca!* (*Castanets click mysteriously among the muffled figures. Music comes from the entrance of the cantina. The thirst-crazed peasant turns that way.*)

THE GUITAR PLAYER. (*As if speaking for him.*) The fountain is dry. But there is wine in the cantina of the Siete Mares. The cellars of the hotel are stocked with wine. (*The PEASANT stumbles toward the hotel. The PROPRIETOR steps out, a lordly fat man in a white linen suit, smoking a cigar and fanning himself with a palm leaf fan. As the PEASANT advances he blows a whistle. A man in military dress steps out of cantina.*)

OFFICER. Go back! (*The MAN stumbles forward. The OFFICER fires at him. He lowers his hands to his stomach, turns slowly about and staggers to the fountain where he falls in a motionless heap. The PROPRIETOR and the OFFICER return inside. The Plaza is silent and motionless again.*)

BLOCK II

> *Someone is heard whistling as he approaches. The sound revives the plaza. Vague movements commence among the STREET FIGURES; they uncover their baskets and arrange their wares: huaraches, silver, peppers, etc. They begin to murmur almost wordlessly among themselves with the weary sound of pigeons.*
>
> *Another moment and the WHISTLER appears. He is a*

young American wanderer about twenty-five. He wears dungarees and a skivvy shirt, the pants, faded nearly white from long wear and much washing, fit him as closely as the clothes of sculpture. He has a pair of golden boxing gloves slung about his neck, his belt is ruby and emerald-studded. He enters from stage right, along the Camino Real.

Stops before the chalked inscription "KILROY IS COMING." Scratches out "COMING" and prints "HERE."

KILROY. (*Very genially, to all present.*) Haha! (*Then he walks up to the* OFFICER *in the dull grey uniform, whose hand tightens on the butt of his revolver as* KILROY *approaches him.*) Buenos Dias, Senor. (*No response—barely a glance.*) Habla Inglesia?
OFFICER. (*Spits, then asks slowly.*) What is it you want?
KILROY. Where is Western Union or Wells-Fargo? I got to send a wire to some friends in the States.
OFFICER. No hay Western Union, no hay Wells-Fargo.
KILROY. That is very peculiar. I never struck a town yet that didn't have one or the other. I just got off a boat. Lousiest frigging tub I ever shipped on, one continual hell it was, all the way up from Rio. And me sick, too. I picked up one of those tropical fevers. No sick-bay on that tub, no doctor, no medicine or nothing, not even one quinine pill, and I was burning up with Christ knows how much fever. I couldn't make them understand I was sick. I got a bad heart, too. I had to retire from the prize ring because of my heart. I was the light heavyweight champion of the West Coast, won these gloves!—before my ticker went bad.— Feel my chest! Go on, feel it! (*He seizes the* OFFICER'S *hand and presses it to his chest.*) Feel it. I've got a heart in my chest as big as the head of a baby. Ha-ha! They stood me in front of a screen that makes you transparent and that's what they seen inside me, a heart in my chest as big as the head of a baby! With something like that you don't need the Gypsy to tell you, "Time is short, Baby—get ready to hitch on wings!" Ha-ha! The medics wouldn't okay me for no more fights, and I was advised to give up smoking and liquor and sex. (*Guitar under softly.*) Ha-ha! To give up sex! —I used to believe a man couldn't live without sex—but he *can* —if he *wants* to! My real true woman, my wife, she would of

46

stuck with me, but it was all spoiled with her being scared and me, too, that a real hard kiss would kill me!—So one night while she was sleeping I wrote her good-bye. . . . Y' know what it is you miss most when you've separated from someone you lived with and loved? It's waking up in the night with that warmness beside you. Once you get used to that warmness, it's a hell of a

(PLAINTIVE MUSIC UNDER.)

lonely feeling to wake up without it, especially in some dollar-a-night hotel room. Ha-ha! A hot water bottle won't do, and a stranger won't do. It has to be someone you're used to and that you know loves you! (*He notices a lack of attention in the* OF-FICER; *grins.*) No comprendo the lingo? (MUSIC OUT.)

OFFICER. What is it you want?

KILROY. (*His spirits visibly flagging.*) Excuse my ignorance but what place is this? What is this country and what is the name of

(MUSIC RESUMES MYSTERIOUS.)

this town? (OFFICER *stares at him in a slight, contemptuous smile*) I know it seems funny of me to ask such a question. Loco! But I was so glad to get off that rotten tub I didn't ask nothing of no one except my pay—and I got short-changed on that. I have trouble counting these pesos or Whatzit-you-call-em. (*Jerks out wallet.*) All-a-this-here. In the States that pile of lettuce would make you a plutocrat!—But I bet you this stuff don't add up to fifty dollars American coin. Ha-ha!

OFFICER. (*Hollowly—mocking.*) Ha-ha.

KILROY. (*Uneasily.*) Ha-ha!

OFFICER. (*Making it sound like a death-rattle.*) Ha-ha-ha-ha-ha. (*He turns and starts in the cantina.* KILROY *grabs his arm.*)

KILROY. Hey!

OFFICER. (*Rather fiercely.*) What is it you want?

KILROY. What is the name of this country and this town? (OF-FICER *thrusts his elbow in* KILROY'S *stomach and twists his arm loose with Spanish curse. Kicks the swinging doors open and enters cantina.*) Brass hats are the same everywhere. (*Soon as the* OFFICER *goes the* STREET PEOPLE *come forward and crowd about* KILROY *with their wheedling cries.*)

(LIGHT MUSIC.)

STREET PEOPLE. Dulces, dulces! Loteria! Loteria! Recuerdos? Recuerdos? Pastele, cafe con leche!

KILROY. No caree, no caree! (*An indescribably frightful old*

47

PROSTITUTE *creeps up to him and grins nightmarishly.*)
PROSTITUTE. Love? Love?
KILROY. *What* did you say?
PROSTITUTE. *Love*
KILROY. No, thanks, I have ideals!
THE GYPSY'S LOUDSPEAKER. Are you perplexed by something? Are you tired out and confused? Do you have a fever? (KILROY *looks a. und for the source of the voice.*) Do you feel yourself to be spiritually unprepared for the age of exploding atoms? Do you distrust the newspapers? Are you suspicious of governments? Have you arrived at a point on the Camino Real where the walls converge not in the distance but right in front of your nose? Does further progress appear impossible to you? Are you afraid of anything at all? Afraid of your heart-beat? Or the eyes of strangers? Afraid of breathing? Afraid of not breathing? Do you wish that things could be straight and simple again as they were in your childhood? Would you like to go back to Kindy Garden! (*The old* PROSTITUTE *has crept up to* KILROY *while he listens. She reaches out to him. At the same time a* PICKPOCKET *lifts his wallet.*)
KILROY. (*Catching the whore's wrist.*) Keep y'r hands off me, y' dirty ole bag! No carne putas! No loteria, no dulces, nada—so get away! Vamoose! All of you! Quit picking at me! (*Reaches in his pocket and jerks out a handful of small copper and silver coins which he flings disgustedly down the street. The grotesque* PEC ' *scramble after it with their inhuman cries.* KILROY *goes on a few steps—then stops short—feeling the back pocket of his dungarees. Then he lets out a startled cry.*) Robbed! By God, I've been robbed! (*The* STREET PEOPLE *scatter to the walls. Turning furiously from one to another.*) Which of you got my wallet? WHICH of you dirty——? Shhhh—— Uh! (*They mumble with gestures of incomprehension. He marches back to entrance to hotel.*) Hey! Officer! Oficial!—General! (*The* OFFICER *finally lounges out of the shadowy hotel entrance and glances at* KILROY *with contempt.*) Tienda? One of them's got my wallet! Picked it out of my pocket while that old whore there was groping me! Don't you comprendo?
OFFICER. (*Slowly.*) Nobody rob you. You don't have no pesos.
KILROY. Huh?
OFFICER. You just dreaming that you have money. You don't ever have money. Nunca! Nada! (*Spits between his teeth.*) Loco . . .

(OFFICER *crosses to fountain.* KILROY *stares at him speechlessly for a moment, then bawls out.*)

KILROY. We'll see what the American Embassy says about this! I'll go to the American Consul! I'll have you all—locked up! Jail! Calaboose! The whole—kit and kaboodle of yuh—dirty—ole—tramps—whores! Leeches! Zopilotes! Snakes!

OFFICER. (*Stopping by the frightful prostitute.*) Pssst! Rosita! (*Jerks his head toward the cantina. She grins horribly and follows him into it. Exhausted by his emotion,* KILROY *leans against wall by hotel. Clutches his pounding heart and pulls out a crumpled blue bandanna to swab his forehead and throat.*)

KILROY. Whew! This deal is rugged! Yes, baby—a rugged deal! (*He slowly crosses the Plaza and goes into the entrance beneath the three brass balls, loosening his ruby and emerald studded belt.*)

BLOCK III

There is a fading of light. First dusk falls on the plaza with an effect of coolness.

At some distance a WOMAN *begins to sing.*

WOMAN.

> "Noche de ronda,
> Que triste pase,
> Que triste cruza—
> Por mi balcon!"

(*The* GUITAR PLAYER *steps suddenly forward and sweeps his strings.*)

PLAYER. The presence of women has softened the speech of the city! (*From inside the Siete Mares there is a rich peal of male laughter. The* PROPRIETOR *steps out upon the street. He is an august gentleman in a light tropical suit, a black string tie, a pith helmet. His voice and manner are suave and unctuous.*)

PROPRIETOR. Forty pesos a day, American plan. We serve distilled water and have the best wine-cellar in the tropics. We provide for the comfort of our guests, but not their safety. Their jewels and valuables should be deposited with the cashier. Acqui se habla Ingles! Ha-ha-ha! (*He takes out a big gold watch and stares at it*

49

fondly. The GUITAR PLAYER *strums softly.* PROPRIETOR, *looking up slowly.*) They are selling the lottery on San Juan de Latrene.

PLAYER. And on the Camino Real.

PROPRIETOR. The girls in the Panama clip-joints are drinking Blue Moons, the gobs and the sea-going bell-hops are getting stewed, screwed and tattooed, and the S. P.'s are busy as cats on a hot tin-roof! Ha ha!—On South Rampart Street and Market Street and Beale Street and Main Street, the nickelodeons and the slot-machines are doing a land-office business. Also the silver screens and the no-cover-charge cantinas, for all work and no play makes Jack a poor jerk who will not get to first base with Jill!

PLAYER. On the Camino Real.

PROPRIETOR. That's right, on the Camino Real! Ha-ha!—You know, to believe in luxury isn't necessarily nor even probably to lack dynamism——

PLAYER. On the Camino Real.

PROPRIETOR. For lots of babies who've never been properly weaned from Hotel Statler room-service, can still make sing or make like magnificent singing—canaries in bed-springs! Ha-ha!

PLAYER. On the Camino Real.

PROPRIETOR. That's right, on the Camino Real!—And in the Loop of Chicago—why, that's the way the crow flies between kids' giggles and light-hearted cohabitation. But, oh, I can tell you!—I have seen them all and known them all and done them all out of their last lucky dollar! Ha-ha!

PLAYER. On the Camino Real.

PROPRIETOR. There's a sort of magnificence in my kind of a robber! I'm a silk-glove artist, and absolutely sincere!

PLAYER. On the Camino Real?

PROPRIETOR. Yes, on the Camino Real! Ha-ha! And my death will be like the fall of a capital city, the sack of Rome or the destruction of Carthage —— And, oh, the memories that will go up in smoke! And you mean to tell me that all this flesh will be lost? Ha-ha! It's a joke! I don't for one moment believe you! But still the street-cleaners have given me sidelong glances, which I pretend to ignore.

PLAYER. On the Camino Real.

PROPRIETOR. For I am the owner of the Siete Mares!

PLAYER. On the Camino Real. (*Music changes to lyrical.*)

PROPRIETOR. (*With an airy gesture.*) In Yboe City the five-point standards are lit. In Guadalajara the colonnades of the plaza are filled with a murmur of girls vending soft-colored drinks, and girls in the tolerant zones are saying the words that pass for love-poems ——

PLAYER. On the Camino Real.

PROPRIETOR. (*Soberly.*) But there is a moment when we look into ourselves and ask with a wonder which never is lost altogether: Can this be all? Is this it? Is this what the glittering wheels of the heavens turn for? (*Then he leans forward as if conveying a secret.*) Ask the Gypsy! *Un poco dinero* will tickle the Gypsy's palm and give her visions! (*Straightens with a huge laugh, clapping his stomach.*)

PLAYER. On the Camino Real!

PROPRIETOR. Yes, on the Camino Real! Ha-ha-ha!

BLOCK IV

> JACQUES *and* MARGUERITE *come out of hotel. She wears white with heaps of pale violets on her hat.*
>
> *They sit at the small round table which bears a sliced papaya and grapes and a tall green bottle and two rose-colored thin-stemmed glasses.*
>
> *A weird piping approaches.* PROPRIETOR *returns outside to listen.*
>
> JACQUES *rises nervously.*

JACQUES. Mr. Gutman, we didn't ask for music!

MARGUERITE. (*Gently.*) Be still, Jacques. You know what it is.

PROPRIETOR. I'm sorry but there isn't much we can do about it. An Indian died of thirst today in the plaza. You see, the springs are dried up and there isn't a drop of water in the fountain and not everybody can afford to buy wine.

JACQUES. Doesn't the government do anything about it?

PROPRIETOR. (*Vaguely.*) Ah, the government! (*Fans himself with a palm leaf fan.*)

JACQUES. What kind of government is it?

PROPRIETOR. Democratic.

JACQUES. Well, I suspect it is really just a big corporation in which a few are stockholders and all the rest—petty wage-slaves!

PROPRIETOR. Does that strike you, sir, as being at all unique?

JACQUES. I have never been in a country, nominally Democratic or anything else, where even the most underprivileged citizen would be permitted to die of thirst in front of an hotel overflowing with wine.

PROPRIETOR. Have you—*travelled*, Senor?

JACQUES. Very widely.

PROPRIETOR. Then I can only assume that you have never looked out of your hotel windows!

MARGUERITE. Be careful, Jacques! (*The* STREET-CLEANERS *enter through arch at top of alley and advance into plaza, trundling their big white barrel on wheels, old German prints of the "Dance of Death" will suggest their appearance, except that they wear white jackets and caps and have brooms. They go to the fountain and kick the prostrate figure over on its back, pick it up and thrust it doubled up in the barrel. Then they lean on their brooms, whispering and giggling and staring at the couple.*) Waiter! (*He approaches.* MARGUERITE, *removing a bill from her purse.*) Give this to the men by the fountain and ask them to please move away. (WAITER *backs away fearfully.*)

PROPRIETOR. It's no use, Madam. Those two are the only public servants in town that are not susceptible to bribes. But don't look at them, only look at each other, and congratulate yourself on having your residence at the Siete Mares. Tonight there will be a fiesta!

MARGUERITE. (*Returning bill to her purse.*) What kind of fiesta?

PROPRIETOR. Whenever there's a full moon, the virginity of the Gypsy's daughter is publicly restored. She dances on the roof and her kinsmen dance in the plaza. It's the main attraction of our tourist season! Do you dance, Senor?

MARGUERITE. Senor Casanova has danced in all the courts of Europe.

PROPRIETOR. If he dances well enough to please the Gypsy's daughter, he might be invited inside—to lift her veil! Ha-ha! But I don't know—it's a doubtful honor! They tell me her mother turns a black card up for the chosen hero! (*Starts inside, laughing.*) Waiter! Bring the lady and gentleman a bottle of Lachrymae Christi with my compliments! And you—player of the blue guitar—*avante!* (*The* LADY *turns full to the audience and her speech is delivered as a recitative with guitar accompaniment. The* PLAYER *stands close beside her and delicately keys his playing to her speech.*)

MARGUERITE. This dusty plaza with its dried-up fountain is like the skeleton of a scene from my youth. In a town of Provence where I once stayed for a summer there was a public fountain where the adolescent boys used to loiter at night. I had a precocious eye for them, at fifteen. It made a difference to me if they were slender and heavier in the shoulders than at the waist. I liked the gleam of white teeth and the attar of roses that some of them oiled their hair with. On a certain night of the week, I believe it was Thursday, it was customary for pairs of girls to walk around the fountain in one direction and pairs of boys in the other, and for the boys to offer bouquets of flowers to girls they wanted to call on. But the boy whose flowers I wanted did not take part in the walking about the fountain. He sat by the edge of the fountain and watched and smiled and the teeth in the Romany darkness of his face, for his father had been a gypsy, shone like a piece cut out of his starched white shirt. His eyes were northern, however, and startlingly blue. But he didn't return my look nor offer me flowers. And when the others had drifted away from the plaza, he still sat there. But then he picked up his guitar, and began to play! (*Bring guitar music up:* ESTRELLITA. *The* LADY *pushes her wine glass toward the bottle with a smile.*)

JACQUES. What is the point of this story?

MARGUERITE. You mean the moral? *Quien sabe!* (*Laughs.*) But wait till it's finished. . . . One summer evening, during the promenade—when I had been offered five or six bunches of flowers and turned them all down, all down!—I suddenly grabbed a bouquet that my friend had accepted . . .

JACQUES. Si?

MARGUERITE. And crossed to the fountain with my heart in my mouth. I went to where he was sitting, the handsome Gitano.— For you, I whispered!—I tossed the flowers toward him . . .

JACQUES. And then?

MARGUERITE. And then I ran home.

JACQUES. Did he call on you?

MARGUERITE. No.

JACQUES. So you languished away?

MARGUERITE. No, indeed.

53

JACQUES. So what did you do?

MARGUERITE. I learned of a path that he took going home late at night when the cantinas had closed.

JACQUES. Ha-ha!

MARGUERITE. I lay in wait for him there. I had a white dress on, I think he must have taken me for a ghost. He crossed himself and whispered the name of God's Mother!—But then I moaned and he knew—that I was—mortal. . . .

JACQUES. Ha-ha-ha!

MARGUERITE. (*Leaning back exultantly.*) That was the night that was talked about in the poem, the one that says that "The stars threw down their spears and watered heaven with their ears!"

JACQUES. They wept with pity because he passed you by?

MARGUERITE. They wept with joy because he—stopped—beside me. . . . (MUSIC: *Tango. A pair of masked* DANCERS *enter the plaza, perform a brief, dramatic dance.* MARGUERITE, *as the dancers retire.*) I have had many loves. (*She drinks.*) But the time which I didn't dare think of, when youth would be lost, is now here. Yes, it's here and I'm here—sitting with someone for whom I have no desire—who has none for me—waiting to watch a young Gypsy dance on a roof—and trying to seem to ignore the ancient street-cleaners' impertinent glances at us! (*She touches his hand.*)

JACQUES. (*Ironically.*) Thank you.

MARGUERITE. We're used to each other. Yes, we've grown used to each other, and that's what passes for love at this far, moonlit end of the Camino Real.

JACQUES. The sort of violets—that can grow on the moon?

MARGUERITE. Or in the crevices of those far-away mountains, among the crevices—fertilized by the droppings of carrion-birds. . . . We're used to each other . . .

JACQUES. And when the street-cleaners approach us, and refuse to be bribed or distracted—when it's unmistakably plain that one of us or the other is being called for—— Couldn't we—both ——?

MARGUERITE. Go together?

JACQUES. Yes.

MARGUERITE. I don't know. I'm afraid to guess, Jacques. When you've spent as much of your heart as I've spent of mine, it's hard to conjecture how much of it may be left. (WAITER *brings wire to gentleman. He reads it and drops his head in his hands.)* What is it?

JACQUES. My remittances are cut off.

MARGUERITE. Completely?

(CANCION: MINOR FAROLITO).

JACQUES. Yes. (MARGUERITE *rises.*) Where are you going?

MARGUERITE. (*Carefully.*) I'm going to get a shawl. The evening comes so quickly and so cold. I can't afford to be chilled.

JACQUES. (*Springing up.*) Marguerite! (MARGUERITE *murmurs something indistinguishable. She enters hotel quickly. The* STREET-CLEANERS *giggle.* WOMAN *resumes song: "Farolito." He slumps back into his seat. The* PROPRIETOR *comes out.*)

PROPRIETOR. I hope you enjoyed your supper.

JACQUES. Yes, thank you.

PROPRIETOR. Oh, by the way, we are having to move you out of your room tonight. There was a mix-up in our reservations.

JACQUES. —Where can I go?

PROPRIETOR. You might try the Casa de Huespedes.

JACQUES. Where?

PROPRIETOR. It's across from the Laboratory. And your luggage is in the lobby. (*Goes back in.* JACQUES *slowly follows. Now the* GUITAR PLAYER *indicates a division of scenes.*)

BLOCK V

KILROY *comes out of the pawn-shop.*

A lighter music.

A foppish elderly man comes out of the cantina. He has on a light suit with a carnation in the lapel. KILROY *starts towards him. Notices the* STREET-CLEANERS. *Snatches up a rock and flings it at them. They dodge the missile and laugh.*

Skirting them widely, KILROY *crosses to the elegant old man.*

KILROY. —Hey, Mac! It's wonderful to see you!

BARON. Really? Why?

KILROY. A normal American in a clean white suit!

55

BARON. My suit is pale yellow, my nationality is French and I am not at all normal—but thanks! Can you give me the time?

KILROY. Nope. My watch is in a pawnshop on South Rampart Street in New Orleans.

BARON. How about a light?

KILROY. I don't smoke.

BARON. You don't have any of the minor vices?

KILROY. I'm strictly a square. But you could do me a favor.

BARON. I'd be charmed to. What is it?

KILROY. Lend me five bucks on my belt!

BARON. Sorry.

KILROY. It's ruby and emerald studded!

BARON. It isn't my sort of thing. But if you should happen to find the time or a light, ask for the Baron de Charlus at the desk. (BARON *enters hotel: the* PROPRIETOR *chuckles.* KILROY *crosses to him.*)

KILROY. —Could you ——?

PROPRIETOR. There's an establishment across the Plaza where loans can be secured on certain collateral.

KILROY. I've just been to the Loan Shark's. All he wanted was my lucky gloves, which I'm not ready to part with.

PROPRIETOR. Better hold on to anything that's lucky, for little compunction is shown to a man without luck along here on the Camino Real.

KILROY. What is the Camino Real?

PROPRIETOR. Everyone has to find that out for himself.

KILROY. Isn't there some way out?

PROPRIETOR. You see that narrow alley that goes by the Gypsy's and passes underneath the crumbling arch? That's The Way Out.

KILROY. I don't like the looks of it.

PROPRIETOR. Neither do I.

KILROY. There's mountains beyond it.

PROPRIETOR. Those mountains are covered with snow.

KILROY. A pair of skis would be useful.

PROPRIETOR. (*Laughs.*) *Very!* Ha-ha-ha! (*The* STREET-CLEANERS *point and giggle.*) I'm afraid you've attracted the attention of the street-cleaning department.

KILROY. What do they do with stiffs picked up in this town?

PROPRIETOR. It's better to have five dollars in your pocket. Otherwise you're removed to the laboratory.

KILROY. What happens there?

PROPRIETOR. You're taken apart. Your vital organs are put in pickle jars! (*Laughs and enters hotel.*)

KILROY. That's no way to treat a human body! (JACQUES *comes out with his luggage.*) Hey, Mac!—As one gringo to another, in this mysterious place whose name isn't mentioned — could you ——?

JACQUES. No, I couldn't. My remittances are cut off, I have just been evicted from the Siete Mares and abandoned by my last friend.

KILROY. Our situations are kind of embarrassing, ain't they? (*Grins and extends his hand.*) I'll see you later! (*Starts across plaza.*) —Buddy! (*He kicks a rock thoughtfully.* JACQUES *moves over.* KILROY *slowly crosses the plaza toward the Loan Shark's, kicking a rock before him, and thoughtfully removing the golden gloves from about his neck. At a motion from the* GUITAR PLAYER, *the* STREET-CLEANERS *withdraw.*)

(CANCION: "NECHE DE RONDA.")

BLOCK VI

PLAYER. Ole! The moon! (*The light changes as the full moon rises above the mountain range. A cool white radiance gilds the plaza. The* WOMAN *sings at a distance, as* INDIANS *in dark blankets enter the plaza with lanterns and baskets covered with snowy clothes.*) Hoy! Noche de fiesta! (*The light falls on the roof of the Gypsy's. On it suddenly appears the* GYPSY'S DAUGHTER. *She throws up her jewelled arms in a harsh flamenco cry. One of the Indians throws aside his blanket revealing a brilliant gypsy costume. He begins to dance. Then another. It is repeated till all the* CROWD *is dancing. On the roof above them the* GYPSY'S DAUGHTER *utters the sharp cries of the flamenco. The music changes. The* GYPSY'S DAUGHTER *begins to dance on the roof, the* OTHERS *falling back to watch—except the* PLAYER *of the blue guitar who stands directly beneath her.* KILROY *comes out of pawnshop, he is drawn across the plaza by her dancing. The* CROWD *divides before him. He comes directly beneath the dancing girl. She looks down at him and stops moving except for her castanets.*) Ole! The Champion of the Golden Gloves! (*He begins to dance, first with rigid movements, then more freely, then with abandon. The* GIRL *utters*

57

the flamenco cries as he dances. At the climax of his dance the GIRL leans over the edge of the roof and tosses her flower to him. There is a great cry from the gathering.) Ole! The Chosen Hero! (KILROY collapses with exhaustion. The male dancers seize him and lift him to their shoulders. There is a burst of fireworks. Roman candles on the roof of the Gypsy, pinwheels about the plaza, triumphal band music. The dancers form a parade, bearing KILROY on their shoulders about the fountain while the girls pelt him with blossoms. He is borne to the door of the Gypsy's establishment and there set down on his feet. KILROY is abashed and a little frightened. He gives the crowd an awkward salute, hoping they will disperse so he can slip quietly away. But they repeat their cheer and crowd closer about him. The door of the Gypsy's opens and a harsh female voice calls out: "PASE USTED!" The crowd echoes: "Pase Usted!" Seeing no way out, KILROY hitches up his belt and slowly advances to the door. He salutes once more, then hesitantly enters: the door slams shut. The loudspeaker on the roof croaks continually like a cracked record: "That's all, that's all, that's all, that's all . . ." VOICE: "Esmeralda, turn that damned thing off!" The loudspeaker squawks, then is silent. The crowd pick up their hats and rebozos and disperse singing in pairs. The plaza is empty except for JACQUES and the FLOWER-VENDOR. JACQUES trails about the plaza, calling faintly:)

JACQUES. Marguerite? Marguerite?

MADRECITA. Flores, flores para los muertos. Corones, corones para los muertos . . .

DIM OUT PLAZA

BLOCK VII

(NOTE: In this scene I am trying to catch the quality of really "tough" Americana of the comic sheets, the skid-row bars, cat-houses, Grade B movies, street-Arabs, vagrants, drunks, pitch-men, gamblers, whores, all the rootless, unstable and highly spirited life beneath the middle-class social level in the States.)

Light up behind scrim at Gypsy's. This scene is one of Oriental or Moorish opulence as it might be dreamed of *by a traveling salesman or drawn by Rube Goldberg, huge tasseled silk pillows, elaborate lamps, incense burners, occult signs and devices and chart of the heavens. There is a low table bearing an illuminated crystal ball. In the back is an alcove curtained off by sheer material. The GYPSY is discovered at a low round table which is covered with a cloth of purple silk, hanging to the floor with fringes of gold braid. On this table is the crystal ball and the deck of cards. She is peering into the crystal with jeweled fingers clasped to her temples.*

KILROY enters through a curtain of beaded strings hanging to the left of the Gypsy. She appears to ignore his presence. He coughs to attract her attention.

GYPSY. Siente se, por favor.

KILROY. No comprendo the lingo.

GYPSY. Yankee?

KILROY. Yankee.

GYPSY. (*Calling to rear.*) Yankee!

VOICE. (*Behind.*) Yankee! (KILROY *laughs uneasily, wiping his brow with bandanna.*)

GYPSY. Name?

KILROY. Kilroy.

GYPSY. Address?

KILROY. Traveller.

GYPSY. Parents?

KILROY. I was brought up by an eccentric old aunt in Toledo.

GYPSY. Childhood diseases?

KILROY. Whooping cough, measles and mumps.

GYPSY. (*Handing him a blank.*) Sign this.

KILROY. What is it?

GYPSY. Just some kind of a blank. You always sign something, don't you?

KILROY. Not till I know what it is.

GYPSY. It's just a little formality to give a tone to the establishment and make an impression on our out-of-town trade. Roll up your sleeve.

KILROY. What for?

GYPSY. A shot of some kind.

59

KILROY. What kind?

GYPSY. Any kind. Don't they always give you some kind of a shot?

KILROY. "They?"

GYPSY. Brass-hats, Americanos! (*Injects hypo.*)

KILROY. I am no guinea pig!

GYPSY. Don't kid yourself. We're all of us guinea-pigs in the laboratory of God. Humanity is just a work in progress.

KILROY. I don't make it out.

GYPSY. Who does? The Camino Real is a funny paper read backwards, only we don't dare think about it much. (*Weird piping outside.* KILROY *shifts nervously on his seat.* GYPSY, *grinning.*) Tired? The altitude makes you sleepy?

KILROY. It makes me nervous.

GYPSY. I'll show you how to take a slug of tequila!—First you sprinkle salt on the back of your hand. Then lick it off with your tongue. Now then you toss the shot down! (*Demonstrates.*)—And then you bite into the lemon. That way it goes down easy, but what a bang!—You're next.

KILROY. No, thanks, I'm on the wagon.

GYPSY. There's an old Chinese proverb that says, "When your goose is cooked you might as well have it cooked with plenty of gravy." (*She laughs unpleasantly.*) —You're not a bad-looking boy. (*Puts on her glasses and moves around the table.*) Sometimes working for the Yankee dollar isn't a painful profession. Have you ever been attracted by older women?

KILROY. Frankly, no, ma'am.

GYPSY. Well, there's a first time for everything.

KILROY. (*Retreating awkwardly.*) That is a subject I cannot agree with you on.

GYPSY. You think I'm an old bag? (KILROY *laughs awkwardly and moves behind table.*) Why are you crossing upstage? Ha-ha-ha! I am just the motherly type. Ain't that right, Esmeralda?

VOICE. (*Behind.*) *Si, Mama!*

GYPSY. Will you take the cards or the crystal?

KILROY. It's—immaterial.

GYPSY. All right, we'll begin with the cards. (*Shuffles and deals.*) Ask me a question.

KILROY. Has my luck run out?

GYPSY. Baby, your luck ran out the day you were born. Another question.

KILROY. Ought I to leave this town?

GYPSY. It don't look to me like you've got much choice in the matter. Take a card. (KILROY *takes one.*) Ace?

KILROY. Yes, ma'am.

GYPSY. What color?

KILROY. Black.

GYPSY. That does it. How big is your heart?

KILROY. As big as the head of a baby.

GYPSY. It's going to break.

KILROY. That's what I was afraid of.

GYPSY. The street-cleaners are waiting for you outside the door.

KILROY. Which door, the front one? I'll slip out back!

GYPSY. It ain't no use. Leave us face it frankly, your number is up. (KILROY *sinks back down thoughtfully.* STREET-CLEANERS' *piping.*)

KILROY. I kind of figured as much. I've had a run of bad luck on the Camino Real. Sometimes you figure your luck is going to quit when you're too lucky and sometimes when luck ain't with you, you figure it's due. But when I landed here I had a feeling that this was the spot marked X on the chart of my life, and that X was not the spot where the treasure was buried. . . .

GYPSY. I like your good sense. You must've known a long time that the name of Kilroy was on the street-cleaners' list.

KILROY. Sure. But not on top of it!

GYPSY. Ha-ha-ha. It's always a bit of a shock. But here's good news. The Queen of Hearts has turned up in the proper position.

KILROY. What's that mean?

GYPSY. Love, Baby!

KILROY. Love?

GYPSY. Uh-huh. The Booby Prize!—Esmeralda!! (*She rises and hits a gong.*) My daughter, Esmeralda! (*A light goes on in the alcove, making the diaphanous drapes transparent. The scene behind them is like a picture on the lid of a cigar box. The GYPSY'S DAUGHTER is seated in a reclining position on a low divan of exotic shape and color. This is the little lady that danced on the roof. She is dressed in a gorgeous minimum of a costume. A spangled veil covers her face and it depends from a silver star on her forehead. From this veil to the girdle, below her navel, that supports her diaphanous bifurcated skirt, she is naked except for a pair of glittering emerald snakes upon her breasts.*)

61

KILROY. (*After an appreciative glance.*) What's *her* specialty? *Tea leaves?*

GYPSY. Ha-ha!—Where is my pistol? I have to go out on the street!

ESMERALDA. You put it in the lower left-hand table drawer, Mama.

GYPSY. Good! I'm going to Walgreen's for change.

KILROY. What change?

GYPSY. The change from that ten-spot you are about to give me. (*Snaps her fingers. He slowly removes a bill.*)

KILROY. How'd you know I had it?

GYPSY. Oh, a little bird told me! (*Winks.*)

KILROY. I hocked my golden gloves to get this saw-buck, so don't go to Hollywood on it.

GYPSY. No one is gypped at the Gypsy's.—Such changeable weather! I'll slip on my summer furs! (*She throws on a greasy blanket and crosses to beaded string curtains.*) Adios! (*She is hardly offstage when two shots ring out.*)

ESMERALDA. (*Plaintively.*) Mother has such an awful time on the street. . . .

KILROY. You mean that she is insulted on the street?

ESMERALDA. Yes, by strangers.

KILROY. Well—I shouldn't think *acquaintances* would do it. (ESMERALDA *curls up on the low divan in the alcove. There is a slight pause in which they regard each other.*)

KILROY. (*Hesitantly.*) Do you—do you like pictures? (ESMERALDA *smiles and blinks rapidly.*) Here is a snapshot of my real true woman! (*Removes thumbed snapshot from wallet and extends to* ESMERALDA. *She takes it with affected interest and stares at it with artificial smile.* KILROY, *sadly.*) You're looking at it up-side down. (ESMERALDA *sighs and returns it to him.*) She was a platinum blonde the same as Jean Harlow. Do you remember Jean Harlow? (ESMERALDA *shakes head.*) No, you wouldn't remember Jean Harlow. It shows you are getting old when you remember Jean Harlow. (*Puts snapshot away.*) . . . They say that Jean Harlow's ashes are kept in a little private cathedral at Forest Lawn. . . . Wouldn't it be wonderful if you could sprinkle them ashes over the ground like seeds, and out of each one would spring another Jean Harlow? And when spring comes you could just walk out and pick them off the bush! (*He grins enthusiastically but* ESMERALDA *yawns, touching her lips delicately with a tiny handkerchief.*) You don't talk much.

ESMERALDA. You want me to talk?

KILROY. Well, that's the way we do things in the States. A little vino, some records on the victrola, some quiet conversation—and then if both parties are in a mood for romance . . . (*Gesture.*)

ESMERALDA. Oh. . . . (*She rises indolently and pours some wine from a slender crystal decanter. Starts victrola playing softly: "Quiereme Mucho." Returns to divan and strikes a voluptuous pose. Watching her movements,* KILROY'S *mouth sags open and waters—he wipes it with bandanna. After a thoughtful pause.*) They say that the monetary system has got to be stabilized all over the world.

KILROY. (*Taking glass.*) Huh?

ESMERALDA. It has to do with some kind of agreement which was made in the woods.

KILROY. Oh.

ESMERALDA. How do you feel about the class-struggle? Do you take sides in that?

KILROY. No.

ESMERALDA. Neither do we, because of the dialectics.

KILROY. The which?

ESMERALDA. Languages with accents, I suppose. But all we hope is that they will not bring the Pope over here and put him in the White House.

KILROY. Who?

ESMERALDA. Oh, the Bolsheviskies, those nasty old things with whiskers. And how do you feel about the Mumbo Jumbo? Do you think they've gotten the Old Man in the bag yet?

KILROY. The Old Man?

ESMERALDA. God. We don't think so. We think there has been so much of the Mumbo Jumbo it's put Him to sleep. (*Giggles.*) What are you thinking about?

KILROY. Those green snakes over your—— What do you wear them for?

ESMERALDA. Oh, so that's what you're really interested in!—
Never mind the class-struggle. The stabilization can go and jump
in a lake! And what do you care if the Old Man likes the Mumbo
Jumbo or not! Your question is, why do I wear the green snakes
over my breasts! (*Delicately.*) Ha-ha!—Well, I will tell you!
Supposedly for protection—but, really, for fun! (KILROY *gets up
slowly.*) What are you going to do?
KILROY. I'm about to establish a beach-head on that sofa. (ESMER-
ALDA *giggles and moves coyly aside, patting the space beside her.*
KILROY, *sitting down gingerly.*) How about—lifting your veil?
ESMERALDA. (*Looking shyly down.*) I can't lift it.
KILROY. Why not?
ESMERALDA. I promised Mother I wouldn't.
KILROY. I thought your mother was the broadminded type.
ESMERALDA. Oh, she is, but you know how mothers are. (*Then
impulsively.*) If you say pretty please you can lift it for me!
KILROY. Awww ——
ESMERALDA. Go on, say it! Say pretty please!
KILROY. No!!
ESMERALDA. Why not?
KILROY. It's silly!
ESMERALDA. Then you can't lift my veil!
KILROY. Oh, all right. Pretty please.
ESMERALDA. Say it again!
KILROY. Pretty please.
ESMERALDA. Now say it once more like you meant it! (*He jumps
up. She grabs his hand.*) Don't go away.
KILROY. You're making a fool out of me.
ESMERALDA. I was just teasing a little. Because you're so cute. Sit
down again, please—pretty please! (*He sits back down.*)
KILROY. What is that wonderful perfume you've got on?
ESMERALDA. Guess!
KILROY. Chanel Number Five?
ESMERALDA. No.
KILROY. Tabu?
ESMERALDA. No.
KILROY. I give up.
ESMERALDA. It's *Noche en Acapulco!* (*Then, plaintively.*) I'm just
dying to go to Acapulco. (*She places her forefinger against his*

chest and wriggles coyly.) I wish that you would take me to Acapulco.

KILROY. (*Groaning.*) It's always like this.

ESMERALDA. What?

KILROY. You Gypsys' daughters are invariably reminded of something without which you cannot do—just when it looks like everything has been fixed!

ESMERALDA. That isn't nice at all. I'm not the gold-digger type. Some girls see themselves in silver foxes. I only see myself in Acapulco!

KILROY. At Todd's place?

ESMERALDA. Oh, no, at the Mirador! Watching those pretty boys dive off the Quebrada!

KILROY. Look again, Baby. Maybe you'll see yourself in Paramount Pictures or having a Singapore Sling at a Statler bar!

ESMERALDA. You're being sarcastic?

KILROY. Nope. Just realistic. Excuse me while I go home. (*She grabs his hand again and purrs like a cat.*)

ESMERALDA. Your hand is cold!

KILROY. The romance is gone and the glamor is dissipated.

ESMERALDA. Ohhhh—*Pobracita!* (*She kisses his fingers.*)

KILROY. All of you Gypsys' daughters have hearts of stone, and I'm not whistling Dixie! But just the same, the night before a man dies, he says, "Pretty please—will you let me lift your veil?"—while the street-cleaners wait for him right outside the door!—Because to be warm for a little longer is life. And love?—That's a four-letter word which is sometimes no better than one you see printed on fences by kids playing hooky from school!—Oh, well—what's the use of complaining? You Gypsy's daughters have ears that only catch sounds like the snap of a gold cigarette case! Or, pretty please, Baby—we're going to Acapulco!

ESMERALDA. *Are* we?

KILROY. Yes! In the morning!

ESMERALDA. Ohhhhh! (*She moves her head in a weaving motion.*) I'm dizzy with joy! My little heart is going pitty-pat!

KILROY. My big heart is going boom-boom! Can I lift your veil now?

ESMERALDA. If you will be gentle.

KILROY. I would not hurt a fly unless it had on leather mittens. (*He touches a corner of her spangled veil. She moans.*)

ESMERALDA. Ohhhh . . .

KILROY. What?

ESMERALDA. (*Louder.*) *Ohhhh!*

KILROY. Why! What's the matter?

ESMERALDA. You are not being gentle!

KILROY. I *am* being gentle.

ESMERALDA. You are *not* being gentle.

KILROY. What was I being, then?

ESMERALDA. Rough!

KILROY. I am *not* being rough.

ESMERALDA. Yes, you *are* being rough. You have to be gentle with me because you're the first.

KILROY. Are you kidding?

ESMERALDA. No.

KILROY. How about all of those other fiestas you've been to?

ESMERALDA. Each one's the first one. That is the wonderful thing about Gypsys' daughters!

KILROY. You can say that again!

ESMERALDA. I don't like you when you're like that.

KILROY. Like what?

ESMERALDA. Cynical and sarcastic.

KILROY. I am sincere.

ESMERALDA. Lots of boys aren't sincere.

KILROY. Maybe they aren't but I am.

ESMERALDA. Everyone says he's sincere, but everyone isn't sincere. If everyone was sincere who says he's sincere there wouldn't be half so many insincere ones in the world and there would be lots, lots, lots more really sincere ones!

KILROY. I think you have got something there. But how about Gypsys' daughters?

ESMERALDA. Huh?

KILROY. Are they one hundred percent in the really sincere category?

ESMERALDA. Well, yes, and no, mostly no! But some of them are for a while if their sweethearts are gentle.

KILROY. Would you believe that I am sincere and gentle?

ESMERALDA. I would believe that you believe that you are. (*Pause.*) For a while. . . .

KILROY. Everything's for a while. For a while is the stuff that dreams are made of, Baby! (*Music under.*) Now?—*Now?*

ESMERALDA. Yes, now, but be gentle!—*gentle.* . . . (*He delicately lifts a corner of her veil. She utters a soft cry. He lifts it further. She cries out again. A bit further. She presses a hand to his chest and leans her head back almost out of his reach. Then with a low moan he seizes her head and draws it forcibly toward him while he slowly and deliberately turns the spangled veil all the way up from her face. Her face, revealed for the first time, is drawn into a look of oblivious and ecstatic pain. Softly, with closed eyes.*) I am sincere, I am sincere, I am sincere!

(RAPTUROUS HARP MUSIC.)

KILROY. I am sincere, I am sincere, I am sincere! (*The music dies out.* KILROY *leans back in an attitude of exhaustion, removing his hand from her veil. She slowly opens her eyes and looks at him with troubled wonder.*)

ESMERALDA. Is that all?

KILROY. I am tired.

ESMERALDA. Already? (*He rises slowly and goes wearily down the three steps from the alcove. He speaks with his back to her.*)

KILROY. I am tired, and full of regret. . . .

ESMERALDA. (*Her face hardening.*) —Oh . . .

KILROY. It wasn't much to give my golden gloves for!

ESMERALDA. You pity yourself?

KILROY. That's right, I pity myself and everybody that goes to the Gypsy's daughter. I pity the world and I pity the God who made it. (*Sits down with his back to her.*)

(SAD MUSIC.)

ESMERALDA. It's always like that as soon as the veil is lifted. They're all so ashamed of having degraded themselves, and their hearts have more regret than a heart can hold!

KILROY. (*Bowing his head to his hands.*) Even a heart that's as big as the head of a baby!

ESMERALDA. You don't even notice how pretty my face is, do you?

KILROY. You look like all Gypsys' daughters, no better, no worse. But as long as you get to go to Acapulco, your cup runneth over with ordinary contentment.

ESMERALDA. —I've never been so insulted in all my life!

(MUSIC OUT.)

KILROY. Oh, yes, you have, Baby. And you'll be insulted worse if you stay in this racket. You'll be insulted so much that it will get to be like water off a duck's back! (*Door slams. The beaded cur-*

tains are drawn apart on the GYPSY. ESMERALDA *lowers her veil
hastily and turns her back to them.* KILROY *pretends not to notice
the* GYPSY'S *entrance. She picks up a little bell and rings it over
his head.*) Okay, Mamacita! I am aware of your presence!

GYPSY. Ha-ha! I was followed three blocks by some awful man!

KILROY. Did you catch him? (*She gives him a playful shove.*)

GYPSY. He ducked into a subway! I waited fifteen minutes outside
the men's room and he never came out!

KILROY. Then you went in?

GYPSY. No! I met a sailor!—The streets are brilliant! (*Throwing
up both hands.*) Have you all been good children? (ESMERALDA
makes a whimpering sound. GYPSY, *knowingly.*) Ohhhh! The pussy
will play while the old mother cat is away? (KILROY *gets up,
hitching his belt.*)

KILROY. Your sense of humor is wonderful, but how about my
change, Mamacita!

GYPSY. What change are you talking about?

KILROY. Are you boxed out of your mind? The change from that
ten-spot you trotted over to Walgreen's?

GYPSY. Ohhhh ——

KILROY. Oh, *what?*

GYPSY. (*Counting on her jewelled fingers.*) Five for the works,
one dollar luxury tax, two for the house percentage and two more
pour la service!—makes *ten!* Didn't I tell you?

KILROY. —What kind of a deal is this?

GYPSY. (*Whipping out her little pearl-handled revolver.*) A rugged
one, Baby!

ESMERALDA. Mama, don't be unkind!

GYPSY. Honey, the gentleman's friends are waiting outside and it
wouldn't be nice to detain him!

KILROY. (*Slowly.*) Okay, Mamacita! Me voy! (*He crosses to the
beaded string curtains. Turns and looks back at the* GYPSY *and*
ESMERALDA. *The weird piping of the* STREET-CLEANERS *is heard
outside.* ESMERALDA *twists a ring on her finger. The* GYPSY *polishes
her fingernails with elaborate unconcern.*) —Sincere?—Sure! Completely!—That's the wonderful thing about Gypsy's daughters!
(*He goes out.* ESMERALDA *raises a wondering fingertip to one eye.
Then cries out in a tone of joyous surprise.*)

ESMERALDA. Look, Mama! Look, Mama! A *tear!* (*The light fades out on the phoney paradise of the Gypsy's. The transparency descends. The light returns to the street.)*

BLOCK VIII

There are three figures in the moonlit plaza as KILROY *emerges from the* GYPSY'S. *The* PLAYER OF THE BLUE GUITAR, *standing by the fountain,* LA MADRECITA, *by the foot of the alley,* JACQUES CASANOVA *at the table before the hotel. He has a glass and a wine bottle. This third area is lighted most.*

KILROY *descends into plaza with manner of scared child entering a dark room.*

MADRECITA. *(Lifting her flowers.)* Flores, flores para los muertos, corones, corones para los muertos?
KILROY. No hay dinero. *(Slips past her, glancing nervously about. Sees the gentleman at the table. Starts toward him. With attempted heartiness that rings flat.)* Hey, Mac! *(*JACQUES *looks up slowly.)* How is your situation? Has it improved?
JACQUES. It has deteriorated to a point at which it is only possible to improve.
KILROY. Ha-ha! That's the way to look at it!
JACQUES. Have a seat. Did you enjoy the fiesta?
KILROY. It was a little more than I bargained for, Mac.
JACQUES. How so?
KILROY. I got mixed up with the daughter of the Gypsy. They seem to be running a sort of high-class clip-joint over there.
JACQUES. Did the ladies impose on your trusting nature?
KILROY. You can say that twice, and still repeat it! *(Piping.)* Have you—uh—seen the street-cleaners—lately?
JACQUES. Not since supper, thank God! Are you expecting them?
KILROY. The Gypsy told me that I was on top of their list.
JACQUES. I can't be very far down on it myself.
KILROY. Maybe our numbers have come up together.
JACQUES. As much as I appreciate your company, sir—I cannot regard that as a happy thought.
KILROY. Then skip it.

JACQUES. I will try to. (*Piping again, somewhat closer.*) It's just wind, you know. The wind in the chimney.

KILROY. Sure!—What are you drinking?

JACQUES. (*Pushing bottle toward him.*) The dregs of a wasted life. The souvenirs of a gentleman of fortune who had talent and energy enough to have been a leader of multitudes but was only a lover of women.

KILROY. Is that so bad?

JACQUES. Not if you're a successful lover, but a successful lover is relatively faithful.

KILROY. And you cheated? (*A minor waltz fades in.*)

JACQUES. I was a wolf. To be a wolf is to be the victim of an emotional impotence, and I have been one of the most insatiable wolves on record. I have scrambled from one bed-chamber to another with shirt-tails always on fire, from girl to girl, like buckets of coal-oil poured on a conflagration, down and down the precipitous alley of life, till I came here, where there's no girl and no bed—and this is my last wine-bottle, presented to me with the compliments of the hotel manager who has just thrown me out on my ear because my remittances are cut off and my lady has left me! The name of the wine is a joke. It is Lachrymae Christi which means the Tears of Christ. He might have wept for me once, but all He could give me now is a groan of disgust. (*Laughs and pours* KILROY *some wine.*)

(MUSIC OUT.)

KILROY. Thanks, Mac. I'm also a has-been. A former champion of the golden gloves. I also used to be a Casanova!

JACQUES. Ah?

KILROY. Do you like to look at pictures?

JACQUES. French ones?

KILROY. No, just girls.

JACQUES. Ah. . . . (KILROY *takes out a collection of ragged snapshots. The piping is heard considerably closer, shrill giggling, moan of wind.*)

KILROY. (*Touching his chest.*) Hear that?

JACQUES. I'm afraid I do, but let's pretend that we don't. Who is this young lady attired for bathing?

KILROY. A cookie I used to cut in San Antone.

JACQUES. Beautiful eyes! And this one?

KILROY. A seventeen-year-old Ginny I had in L. A.

70

JACQUES. Milk-fed chicken! This one?

KILROY. I shacked up with her at the Sherman Hotel in Chicago. (*Giggle and piping very close.* KILROY *springs up.* KILROY *hoarsely.*) That's them, the street-cleaners!

JACQUES. Sit down, sit down, Chicquito! Who are these nymphs?

KILROY. (*Very nervously.*) Betsy Lou and Martha Jane Thompkins, identical twins, in Omaha, Nebraska.

JACQUES. Who was lucky Piere?

KILROY. Ha-ha!—Here's my real true woman.

JACQUES. The prettiest of the lot!

KILROY. Yeah, she was my wife. I married her eight years ago, the night after I knocked out the Monterrey killer.

JACQUES. You lucky dog! I never had a wife. (*Piping.* KILROY *starts up again.* CASANOVA *touches his shoulder. He sinks back nervously in his seat.*) Was she faithful to you?

KILROY. Sure she was.

JACQUES. But you grew tired of her?

KILROY. *Never!* It was for *her* sake I quit her. . . . (*Giggle, considerably closer.*) Yeh, *they're* coming!

JACQUES. *Shhh!* The excitement would always pass for me too quickly. They say it comes back again, if you're patient enough. And that's when the really wonderful part commences, when love is not just a rented room—but a home that you can rest in! Where you can unpack your books and hang your pictures! (KILROY *has slumped in his chair a little.*) What is the matter?

KILROY. I have trouble—breathing. . . .

JACQUES. Don't be frightened!—Who is this young lady?

KILROY. (*In painful gasps.*) That's—Vivian! I met her on Benefit Street—in Providence—Rhode Island. (*The piping is now continuous and quite near.*) Will you—hold my hand—please?

JACQUES. (*Softly.*) Going?

KILROY. *Si! Me Voy!* (CASANOVA *takes his hand and embraces his sagging shoulders.*)

JACQUES. (*Gently.*) Isn't it silly? We two old Casanovas, holding hands!

KILROY. (*Breathlessly.*) Ha-ha!

JACQUES. Like a pair of timid old maids at the sound of a mouse in the woodwork!

KILROY. Ha-ha!

JACQUES. Ha-ha-ha!

KILROY. Ha-ha-ha-ha! (*He suddenly pitches over and falls to the street.* STREET-CLEANERS *enter through arch and advance down the alley.* JACQUES *falls slowly back from the table and flattens himself against the wall of the Siete Mares as the frightful figures approach with their giggles and piping. They come up to* KILROY'S *fallen body. Search the pockets. They double him up and stuff him into the barrel. They start off. One of them notices* JACQUES *and points.*)

STREET-CLEANER. Buenos noces, Senor Casanova! (*The other* STREET-CLEANER *giggles mockingly.* JACQUES *averts his face to the wall. They trundle their barrel off into left wings, where a sign points:* "*To the Laboratory.*")

LA MADRECITA. Flores, flores, para los muertos? Corones, corones para los muertos? (JACQUES *returns slowly to the table and finds the wine bottle empty. The* PLAYER OF THE GUITAR *strikes a chord and the scene dims out except for a faint spot of light on* LA MADRECITA *with her gaudy tin flowers.*)

BLOCK IX

Two areas are spotted, one upstage at the foot of the Alley Way out. In this area is seated the old woman flower-vendor, and across her knees, in the attitude of Michelangelo's Pieta, is the body of KILROY.

The other lighted area is downstage center where a low white table on wheels bears a sheeted figure. Beside the table stands a medical instructor addressing a pair of STUDENTS, *all in white surgical jackets.*

INSTRUCTOR. This is the body of an unidentified vagrant.

MADRECITA. This was thy son, America—and now mine.

INSTRUCTOR. He was found in an alley along the Camino Real.

MADRECITA. He had blue eyes and the body of a champion boxer.

INSTRUCTOR. There is no external evidence of disease. There are no marks of violence on the body.

MADRECITA. He had the soft voice of the South, and a pair of golden gloves—but the deal was rugged.

INSTRUCTOR. His death was apparently due to natural causes. (STU-DENTS *make notes. Keening voices.*)

MADRECITA. Yes, blow wind where night thins! He had many loves, many loves. . . .

INSTRUCTOR. In the absence of legal claimants, no friends or relatives having identified him ——

MADRECITA. He stood as a planet among the moons of their longing, haughty with youth, a champion of the prize-ring! You should have seen the lovely, monogrammed robe in which he strode the aisles of the Colisseums!

INSTRUCTOR. After elapse of a certain number of days, his body becomes the property of the State ——

MADRECITA. Yes, blow wind where night thins—for laurel is not everlasting. . . .

INSTRUCTOR. And now is transferred to our hands for the nominal sum of five dollars.

MADRECITA. This was thy son, America—and now mine. . . .

INSTRUCTOR. We will now proceed with the dissection. Knife, please!

MADRECITA. Blow, wind! (*Sound of wind, keening voices.*) Yes, blow wind where night thins! You are his passing bell and his lamentation!

VOICES. Ay, ay, ay! (STUDENT *crosses to* DOCTOR *with knife.*)

MADRECITA. Keen for him all maimed creatures, deformed and mutilated—his homeless ghost is your own!

INSTRUCTOR. First we will open up the chest cavity and examine the heart for evidence of coronary occlusion.

MADRECITA. His heart was pure gold and as big as the head of a baby.

INSTRUCTOR. We will make an incision along the vertical line.
(SOUND: WIND.)

MADRECITA. (*Touching* KILROY'S *forehead with her flowers.*) Rise, ghost! Go, bird! "Humankind cannot bear very much reality." (*At the touch of her flowers,* KILROY *stirs and pushes himself slowly up from the lap of the* MADRECITA. *He rubs his eyes, then springs to his feet and looks around him.*)

VOICES. Ole! Ole! Ole! The chosen hero! (*The* MADRECITA *makes a gesture of benediction. She then turns and passes slowly up the alley.*)

KILROY. Hey! Hey, somebody! Where am I? (*He notices the lighted area of the dissection room and approaches slowly.*)

DOCTOR. (*Removing a glittering sphere from the dummy corpse.*) Look at this heart. It's as big as the head of a baby.

KILROY. (*Indignantly.*) My heart!?

DOCTOR. Put it in the basin and wash it off so we can look for the pathological lesions.

KILROY. (*Awestruck.*) Yes, siree, that's my heart! (*He pauses just outside the lighted area as a* STUDENT *takes the heart and dips it into a basin on stand beside table, suddenly cries out and holds aloft a glittering gold sphere.*)

STUDENT. Hey, Doc! This heart's solid gold! (*Drums, cymbals, other festive noises.*)

KILROY. (*Rushing forward.*) That's mine, you bastards! (*He snatches the gold heart from the student and dashes into right wings.*)

INSTRUCTOR. Stop, thief! Stop, corpse! (*They all pursue* KILROY *offstage.*)

BLACKOUT

BLOCK X

Faint light before daybreak.

ESMERALDA *appears on the* GYPSY'S *roof, enveloped in a diaphanous scarf sprinkled with iridescent silver stars. She stands there like a somnambulist, eyes closed and lips slightly parted in a childish smile.*

KILROY *enters from right wings. Sees* ESMERALDA *and whistles. She gives no sign of attention.*

The music of the Fiesta scene is revived in a ghostly key, much softer, as if played at a distance.

The Fiesta DANCERS *enter. They are all in ghostly white costumes and their faces covered with neo-classic white masks. A spectral ballet is performed to the eerie music.* KILROY *then performs a solo dance directly under the roof.* ESMERALDA *remains with closed eyes. Finally he tosses his heart in the air to catch her attention, and calls her name.*

74

KILROY. Hey! Esmeralda!

ESMERALDA. (*Without looking down.*) Go away, cat!

DANCERS. (*Mockingly.*) Ole! The Chosen Hero! (*They scatter from the stage with mocking laughter.* KILROY *is momentarily baffled. Then a happy thought strikes him and he dashes over to the Loan Shark's and bangs at the door. It opens instantly and the interior lights up.*)

KILROY. (*Entering.*) Quanto por mi corazon? Un corazon de oro! (THE GUITAR PLAYER *strolls out of the cantina, followed by the*
(SONG: ESTRELLITA.)

WOMAN SINGER. *They cross to the* GYPSY'S *and serenade* ESMER-ALDA. *She dances dreamily on the roof.* KILROY *comes back out laden with articles procured in exchange for his heart. A fur coat, a gown of sequins, ropes of pearls, a rhinestone tiara—a fistful of colored pasteboard tickets, a doll with golden curls and a bunch of balloons. He dashes over to point beneath where* ESMERALDA *is standing.*) Hey! Esmeralda!

ESMERALDA. (*Without looking down.*) Go away, cat! Go away, cat!

KILROY. Look who's here! Me! Kilroy!

ESMERALDA. Go away, cat!

KILROY. Aw, don't be sore! I didn't mean to insult you! You misunderstood me, honey. Now look what I've got. Tickets to Acapulco and everywhere else! A real mink coat that was worn by Hedy LaMarr! Hey! Look! (*He releases the colored balloons. They float directly past her. She stretches out her arms.*)

ESMERALDA. Oh, how pretty! (*Then, sadly.*) They're gone. (*She turns and disappears from the roof.* KILROY *drops his presents on the street and rushes up to the* GYPSY'S *door and bangs with both fists. The door is thrown open. A pail of water is thrown into his face.*)

GYPSY. Scat! (*The door slams shut. He backs down into the alley, gasping and spluttering.*)

KILROY. (*In final disgust.*) How do you like them apples! (*A faint, weird music commences. It seems to come from the cantina. The swinging doors push open on a remarkable figure. It is a tall, lank figure dressed as a knight of chivalry, silver armor which is loose and rusty. But the plume on his helmet is downy and white as snow in the rosy light from the cantina's entrance. As he advances with stately, clanking stride, his face also catches the light.*

*It is long and lean and weatherbeaten, and the very wide open
eyes are immensely grave in the old and haunted red face.* KILROY,
still facing the GYPSY'S.) The hell with all of you phoney Gypsys'
daughters. (*The* ANCIENT KNIGHT *stops near* KILROY. *As the down-
cast youth turns toward him, the* KNIGHT'S *face softens into a
smile.*)

KNIGHT. *Que paso, mi amigo?*

KILROY. The deal is rugged! Do you know what I mean?

KNIGHT. Who knows better than I what a rugged deal is! But will
you take some advice?

KILROY. I'll take anything at this point.

KNIGHT. Don't—pity—your—self! (*He touches* KILROY'S *chest with
his long forefinger.*) Ha-ha! The wounds of the vanity, the many
offenses our egos have to endure —— Being housed in bodies that
age, and hearts that grow tired—are better accepted with a tolerant smile—like this! Y'see? (*He stretches his weatherbeaten face
into an enormous grin.*) Otherwise what you become is a bag full
of curdled cream—*leche mala* we call it!—attractive to nobody,
least of all to yourself.

KILROY. —*Who* are you?

KNIGHT. Quixote. Quixote de la Mancha!—Heard of me?

KILROY. Sort of—somewhere, I think.

KNIGHT. Have y' got any plans?

KILROY. No, sir.

KNIGHT. Then come along with me!

KILROY. *Donde?*

KNIGHT. *Quien sabe!*—Who cares!

KILROY. (*After a slight reflection.*) *Como no* —— (*Crosses to sign
"KILROY IS HERE," scratches out "IS" and prints "WAS."*)

KNIGHT. Sancho!

SANCHO. Si, Senor! Si—Senor. . . .

KNIGHT. Ha-ha! *Vaminos!* (*They lock arms and start up the steep
alley together. Bring light up on table before Siete Mares where*
JACQUES *is seated with his head in his arms.* MARGUERITE *appears
at the other side of the plaza. She crosses to the table. He looks
up slowly and slowly rises.*)

JACQUES. I thought you had left me forever.

MARGUERITE. I've only been looking at silver.

JACQUES. They've locked me out of my room.

MARGUERITE. It's all right. I'll take you to mine. Why, Jacques—

you're crying! (*She sinks into chair. He crouches at her feet and buries his face in her lap.* MARGUERITE, *touching his head.*) The violets in the mountains are breaking the rocks!

KNIGHT. (*At the top of the alley.*) Hey! Sancho! Sancho Panza! (*They pause under the crumbling arch.* SANCHO PANZA *stumbles out of the cantina of the Siete Mares, rubber-legged and wobbling under a load of durious knightly equipment.*)

SANCHO. So, Senor! Si—Senor. . . .

QUIXOTE (KNIGHT). (*Passionately.*) *Vaminos!*

SANCHO. (*Wearily.*) *Si, Senor. Me voy, Senor.—Me—voy* . . . (*He turns a bit dizzily. Then starts up the alley way out. The music rises tenderly and richly as the* PLAYER OF THE BLUE GUITAR *steps into the moonlit plaza. A* WOMAN *sings at a distance. He looks about him. Then stretches his arms in a gesture of wonder and finality.*)

THE END

NEW PLAYS

★ **MONTHS ON END by Craig Pospisil.** In comic scenes, one for each month of the year, we follow the intertwined worlds of a circle of friends and family whose lives are poised between happiness and heartbreak. "...a triumph...these twelve vignettes all form crucial pieces in the eternal puzzle known as human relationships, an area in which the playwright displays an assured knowledge that spans deep sorrow to unbounded happiness." *–Ann Arbor News.* "...rings with emotional truth, humor...[an] endearing contemplation on love...entertaining and satisfying." *–Oakland Press.* [5M, 5W] ISBN: 0-8222-1892-5

★ **GOOD THING by Jessica Goldberg.** Brings us into the households of John and Nancy Roy, forty-something high-school guidance counselors whose marriage has been increasingly on the rocks and Dean and Mary, recent graduates struggling to make their way in life. "...a blend of gritty social drama, poetic humor and unsubtle existential contemplation..." *–Variety.* [3M, 3W] ISBN: 0-8222-1869-0

★ **THE DEAD EYE BOY by Angus MacLachlan.** Having fallen in love at their Narcotics Anonymous meeting, Billy and Shirley-Diane are striving to overcome the past together. But their relationship is complicated by the presence of Sorin, Shirley-Diane's fourteen-year-old son, a damaged reminder of her dark past. "...a grim, insightful portrait of an unmoored family..." *–NY Times.* "MacLachlan's play isn't for the squeamish, but then, tragic stories delivered at such an unrelenting fever pitch rarely are." *–Variety.* [1M, 1W, 1 boy] ISBN: 0-8222-1844-5

★ **[SIC] by Melissa James Gibson.** In adjacent apartments three young, ambitious neighbors come together to discuss, flirt, argue, share their dreams and plan their futures with unequal degrees of deep hopefulness and abject despair. "A work...concerned with the sound and power of language..." *–NY Times.* "...a wonderfully original take on urban friendship and the comedy of manners—a *Design for Living* for our times..." *–NY Observer.* [3M, 2W] ISBN: 0-8222-1872-0

★ **LOOKING FOR NORMAL by Jane Anderson.** Roy and Irma's twenty-five-year marriage is thrown into turmoil when Roy confesses that he is actually a woman trapped in a man's body, forcing the couple to wrestle with the meaning of their marriage and the delicate dynamics of family. "Jane Anderson's bittersweet transgender domestic comedy-drama ...is thoughtful and touching and full of wit and wisdom. A real audience pleaser." *–Hollywood Reporter.* [5M, 4W] ISBN: 0-8222-1857-7

★ **ENDPAPERS by Thomas McCormack.** The regal Joshua Maynard, the old and ailing head of a mid-sized, family-owned book-publishing house in New York City, must name a successor. One faction in the house backs a smart, "pragmatic" manager, the other faction a smart, "sensitive" editor and both factions fear what the other's man could do to this house—and to them. "If Kaufman and Hart had undertaken a comedy about the publishing business, they might have written *Endpapers*...a breathlessly fast, funny, and thoughtful comedy ...keeps you amused, guessing, and often surprised...profound in its empathy for the paradoxes of human nature." *–NY Magazine.* [7M, 4W] ISBN: 0-8222-1908-5

★ **THE PAVILION by Craig Wright.** By turns poetic and comic, romantic and philosophical, this play asks old lovers to face the consequences of difficult choices made long ago. "The script's greatest strength lies in the genuineness of its feeling." *–Houston Chronicle.* "Wright's perceptive, gently witty writing makes this familiar situation fresh and thoroughly involving." *–Philadelphia Inquirer.* [2M, 1W (flexible casting)] ISBN: 0-8222-1898-4

DRAMATISTS PLAY SERVICE, INC.
440 Park Avenue South, New York, NY 10016 212-683-8960 Fax 212-213-1539
postmaster@dramatists.com www.dramatists.com

NEW PLAYS

★ **BE AGGRESSIVE by Annie Weisman.** Vista Del Sol is paradise, sandy beaches, avocado-lined streets. But for seventeen-year-old cheerleader Laura, everything changes when her mother is killed in a car crash, and she embarks on a journey to the Spirit Institute of the South where she can learn "cheer" with Bible belt intensity. "…filled with lingual gymnastics…stylized rapid-fire dialogue…" *–Variety.* "…a new, exciting, and unique voice in the American theatre…" *–BackStage West.* [1M, 4W, extras] ISBN: 0-8222-1894-1

★ **FOUR by Christopher Shinn.** Four people struggle desperately to connect in this quiet, sophisticated, moving drama. "…smart, broken-hearted…Mr. Shinn has a precocious and forgiving sense of how power shifts in the game of sexual pursuit…He promises to be a playwright to reckon with…" *–NY Times.* "A voice emerges from an American place. It's got humor, sadness and a fresh and touching rhythm that tell of the loneliness and secrets of life…[a] poetic, haunting play." *–NY Post.* [3M, 1W] ISBN: 0-8222-1850-X

★ **WONDER OF THE WORLD by David Lindsay-Abaire.** A madcap picaresque involving Niagara Falls, a lonely tour-boat captain, a pair of bickering private detectives and a husband's dirty little secret. "Exceedingly whimsical and playfully wicked. A top-drawer production." *–NY Times.* "Full frontal lunacy is on display. A most assuredly fresh and hilarious tragicomedy of marital discord run amok…absolutely hysterical…" *–Variety.* [3M, 4W (doubling)] ISBN: 0-8222-1863-1

★ **QED by Peter Parnell.** Nobel Prize-winning physicist and all-around genius Richard Feynman holds forth with captivating wit and wisdom in this fascinating biographical play that originally starred Alan Alda. "QED is a seductive mix of science, human affections, moral courage, and comic eccentricity. It reflects on, among other things, death, the absence of God, travel to an unexplored country, the pleasures of drumming, and the need to know and understand." *–NY Magazine.* "Its rhythms correspond to the way that people—even geniuses—approach and avoid highly emotional issues, and it portrays Feynman with affection and awe." *–The New Yorker.* [1M, 1W] ISBN: 0-8222-1924-7

★ **UNWRAP YOUR CANDY by Doug Wright.** Alternately chilling and hilarious, this deliciously macabre collection of four bedtime tales for adults is guaranteed to keep you awake for nights on end. "Engaging and intellectually satisfying…a treat to watch." *–NY Times.* "Fiendishly clever. Mordantly funny and chilling. Doug Wright teases, freezes and zaps us." *–Village Voice.* "Four bite-size plays that bite back." *–Variety.* [flexible casting] ISBN: 0-8222-1871-2

★ **FURTHER THAN THE FURTHEST THING by Zinnie Harris.** On a remote island in the middle of the Atlantic secrets are buried. When the outside world comes calling, the islanders find their world blown apart from the inside as well as beyond. "Harris winningly produces an intimate and poetic, as well as political, family saga." *–Independent (London).* "Harris' enthralling adventure of a play marks a departure from stale, well-furrowed theatrical terrain." *–Evening Standard (London).* [3M, 2W] ISBN: 0-8222-1874-7

★ **THE DESIGNATED MOURNER by Wallace Shawn.** The story of three people living in a country where what sort of books people like to read and how they choose to amuse themselves becomes both firmly personal and unexpectedly entangled with questions of survival. "This is a playwright who does not just tell you what it is like to be arrested at night by goons or to fall morally apart and become an aimless yet weirdly contented ghost yourself. He has the originality to make you feel it." *–Times (London).* "A fascinating play with beautiful passages of writing…" *–Variety.* [2M, 1W] ISBN: 0-8222-1848-8

DRAMATISTS PLAY SERVICE, INC.
440 Park Avenue South, New York, NY 10016 212-683-8960 Fax 212-213-1539
postmaster@dramatists.com www.dramatists.com

NEW PLAYS

★ **SHEL'S SHORTS by Shel Silverstein.** Lauded poet, songwriter and author of children's books, the incomparable Shel Silverstein's short plays are deeply infused with the same wicked sense of humor that made him famous. "…[a] childlike honesty and twisted sense of humor." –*Boston Herald.* "…terse dialogue and an absurdity laced with a tang of dread give [*Shel's Shorts*] more than a trace of Samuel Beckett's comic existentialism." –*Boston Phoenix.* [flexible casting] ISBN: 0-8222-1897-6

★ **AN ADULT EVENING OF SHEL SILVERSTEIN by Shel Silverstein.** Welcome to the darkly comic world of Shel Silverstein, a world where nothing is as it seems and where the most innocent conversation can turn menacing in an instant. These ten imaginative plays vary widely in content, but the style is unmistakable. "…[*An Adult Evening*] shows off Silverstein's virtuosic gift for wordplay…[and] sends the audience out…with a clear appreciation of human nature as perverse and laughable." –*NY Times.* [flexible casting] ISBN: 0-8222-1873-9

★ **WHERE'S MY MONEY? by John Patrick Shanley.** A caustic and sardonic vivisection of the institution of marriage, laced with the author's inimitable razor-sharp wit. "…Shanley's gift for acid-laced one-liners and emotionally tumescent exchanges is certainly potent…" –*Variety.* "…lively, smart, occasionally scary and rich in reverse wisdom." –*NY Times.* [3M, 3W] ISBN: 0-8222-1865-8

★ **A FEW STOUT INDIVIDUALS by John Guare.** A wonderfully screwy comedy-drama that figures Ulysses S. Grant in the throes of writing his memoirs, surrounded by a cast of fantastical characters, including the Emperor and Empress of Japan, the opera star Adelina Patti and Mark Twain. "Guare's smarts, passion and creativity skyrocket to awesome heights…" –*Star Ledger.* "…precisely the kind of good new play that you might call an everyday miracle…every minute of it is fresh and newly alive…" –*Village Voice.* [10M, 3W] ISBN: 0-8222-1907-7

★ **BREATH, BOOM by Kia Corthron.** A look at fourteen years in the life of Prix, a Bronx native, from her ruthless girl-gang leadership at sixteen through her coming to maturity at thirty. "…vivid world, believable and eye-opening, a place worthy of a dramatic visit, where no one would want to live but many have to." –*NY Times.* "…rich with humor, terse vernacular strength and gritty detail…" –*Variety.* [1M, 9W] ISBN: 0-8222-1849-6

★ **THE LATE HENRY MOSS by Sam Shepard.** Two antagonistic brothers, Ray and Earl, are brought together after their father, Henry Moss, is found dead in his seedy New Mexico home in this classic Shepard tale. "…His singular gift has been for building mysteries out of the ordinary ingredients of American family life…" –*NY Times.* "…rich moments …Shepard finds gold." –*LA Times.* [7M, 1W] ISBN: 0-8222-1858-5

★ **THE CARPETBAGGER'S CHILDREN by Horton Foote.** One family's history spanning from the Civil War to WWII is recounted by three sisters in evocative, intertwining monologues. "…bittersweet music—[a] rhapsody of ambivalence…in its modest, garrulous way…theatrically daring." –*The New Yorker.* [3W] ISBN: 0-8222-1843-7

★ **THE NINA VARIATIONS by Steven Dietz.** In this funny, fierce and heartbreaking homage to *The Seagull*, Dietz puts Chekhov's star-crossed lovers in a room and doesn't let them out. "A perfect little jewel of a play…" –*Shepherdstown Chronicle.* "…a delightful revelation of a writer at play; and also an odd, haunting, moving theater piece of lingering beauty." –*Eastside Journal (Seattle).* [1M, 1W (flexible casting)] ISBN: 0-8222-1891-7

DRAMATISTS PLAY SERVICE, INC.
440 Park Avenue South, New York, NY 10016 212-683-8960 Fax 212-213-1539
postmaster@dramatists.com www.dramatists.com